Rendering Real and Imagined Buildings

The Art of Computer Modeling

From The Palace of Kublai Khan
to Le Corbusier's Villas

B. J. Novitski

Foreword by
William J. Mitchell

GLOUCESTER MASSACHUSETTS

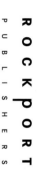

ROCKPORT PUBLISHERS

Windows/Macintosh Interactive CD-ROM
Sketches, Walk-throughs, and Animations

First published in the United States of America by:
Rockport Publishers, Inc.
33 Commercial Street
Gloucester, Massachusetts 01930-5089
Telephone: (978) 282-9590
Facsimile: (978) 283-2742

Manufactured in China

Distributed to the book trade and art trade
in the United States by:
North Light Books, an imprint of
F & W Publications
1507 Dana Avenue
Cincinnati, Ohio 45207
Telephone: (800) 289-0963

Other Distribution by:
Rockport Publishers, Inc.
Gloucester, Massachusetts 01930-5089

ISBN 1-56496-511-2

10 9 8 7 6 5 4 3 2 1

Design: Argus Visual Communication, Boston

End-User License Agreement

Acknowledgments

This book would have remained "unbuilt" without the contributions of dozens of architects, archaeologists, anthropologists, historians, architecture professors, and students. They sent material from Europe, Asia, and all over North America and speak the universal languages of architectural design and computer graphics. They all share a love of building and a belief in the ability of computer technology to bring to life nonexistent architecture. For their support, I particularly want to thank Richard Buday, Glenn Goldman, Karen Kensek, William Mitchell, Donna Matthews, Kevin Matthews, and Thomas Seebohm. And for his special, enduring contributions, love and gratitude to Chip Kiger.

Contents

Foreword:
The Uses of Photorealism

How are we to understand the compelling computer-generated images in this book? What are their uses? By what standards should we judge them?

Many of them, of course, display great technical virtuosity; they illustrate that the technologies of three-dimensional geometric modeling, photorealistic image synthesis, and graphic display have now reached extremely high levels of sophistication. But demonstrations of technological prowess are not ends in themselves—except, perhaps, for CAD software vendors. To obtain deeper and more interesting answers to these questions, we must address some issues of ontology, epistemology, and scholarly responsibility. Do the depicted scenes exist, or are they simply fictions or falsehoods? If they do exist, what can we reliably know about them? How far can we trust the depictions that we are offered? And what scholarly standards should we apply in judging these modeling and visualization efforts?

Reports

To open up these issues, let us consider the most straightforward case first—that of computer-generated architectural views that function as reports on currently existing buildings. Much like photographs, they record and present facts about the physical world.

The production process is very different from that of photographs, of course. First, a three-dimensional (3D) model is captured by traditional means of measurement, through use of photogrammetric methods, or by application of advanced 3D scanning techniques (the larger-scale equivalents of 3D medical imaging techniques, such as magnetic resonance imaging). Next, a viewpoint and lighting conditions are specified. Finally, rendering software is employed to produce a shaded perspective image.

Generally, in this case, we demand care and accuracy in reporting. We expect use of measurement processes that keep errors to an acceptable minimum. Just as with news photographs and medical and scientific images, we require the data to be presented without manipulation. We want the images to be produced according to agreed-upon and understood rendering conventions, not ones that distort the facts. And the results should stand up to direct comparisons with photographs or with the physical reality itself. If these conditions are not met, then we are justified in regarding purported visual reports as sloppy or dishonest evidence and in worrying that they may deceive us.

Why bother with all this when you can just take a snapshot? One justification for the effort is that a 3D model is far more versatile than a photographic negative; it allows us, for example, to produce images from multiple viewpoints and under many different lighting conditions. And a related advantage is that decisions about viewpoint, framing, lighting, and so on can shift from the creator of the information to the computer-equipped user, who may have very different purposes and needs. In the future, as the technology develops, we can probably expect a general shift from image-capture to model-capture techniques; this has already taken place, to a large extent, in medical imaging.

This versatility yields some disconcerting paradoxes, though. Whereas photographs are always unambiguously snapped at particular times and places, a photorealistic computer rendering may be taken from a viewpoint where no human observer ever set foot. Furthermore, evidence of the rendering's purported point in time—such as sun position, surface patina indicating a building's age, and telltale details of entourage—may specify a moment when no observer could possibly have been present.

Despite the visual similarities, then, there are crucial differences between architectural photographs and photorealistic computer-generated renderings of actual scenes. An architectural photograph is a kind of souvenir; it implies that an identifiable individual observer was there, on the spot, at some definite moment. Somebody actually bore witness to the recorded scene, and we can hold that witness accountable for the accuracy of the visual evidence that he or she captures and presents. But a photorealistic computer rendering has no such simple, automatic embedding in geographic and historical reality. In this case, the "witness" is nothing more than a necessary fiction.

Reconstructions

Other scenes in this book depict buildings and urban areas that once physically existed but were subsequently altered or destroyed. The function of the images is to make experientially available to us something that has been lost.

Here, the base information may derive from multiple sources. Some of it may result from on-site surveys of remains. And some—or even all, in the case of complete destruction—may be extracted from contemporary drawings, photographs, or written texts. At the very least, this information must be collated, cross-checked, and organized to create a 3D model.

In most cases, though, the available information will turn out to be incomplete. It may also contain errors and inaccuracies. Thus the modeler must undertake the scholarly task of filling in missing information and resolving problems in the base data. This is an intellectual enterprise closely analogous to that of a textual scholar attempting to recreate a definitive version of some ancient text from the multiple, imperfect, incomplete copies that have come down to us.

Another difficulty is that buildings do, of course, change over time; they weather and decay, and they may be reconstructed and altered in various ways. To complicate matters further, the available evidence about their histories may date from many different points in time. So reconstruction may require creation not just of one 3D model but of lengthy sequences of models. Sometimes, fully sorting out the stages and transitions in a building's life proves to be a very demanding job.

When we judge the results of this sort of modeling process, we must ask whether the conclusions are justified by the available evidence, whether they are consistent with our general knowledge of the context, and whether the author has exhibited sound scholarly judgment in collecting and considering evidence. Certainty tends to be elusive; often there is room for considerable doubt. The outcome, then, may not be a single 3D model but multiple alternatives with different narratives and degrees of likelihood attached.

These ambiguities and uncertainties create dilemmas at the rendering stage, as full photorealism demands complete and detailed specification of geometry and surface properties, whether or not they are all based on firm and complete evidence. As a result, all parts of a rendered scene may appear equally realistic and convincing, even though some may actually be far more conjectural than others. A very similar problem arises in physical reconstruction of ancient ruins, where actual remains must be blended with new construction to recreate the whole. In both cases, the ethical difficulty may be resolved—at some cost to verisimilitude—by abandoning attempts at seamless photorealism and making clear visual distinctions between the actual and the conjectural. The conjectural portions may be shown in a neutral color, for example, while the actual portions are depicted in full color and detail.

Counterfactuals

Yet other images in these pages show buildings that were designed but never constructed. They are visual counterfactuals—depictions of scenes that might have been.

Here, the closest analogy is to performance of hitherto unheard musical compositions or plays that never made it to the stage. Some document that specifies the work exists, and the task is faithfully to instantiate that work so that the experience becomes directly available to an audience. But in this case the instance is to be in the form of a 3D computer model and its visual renditions rather than in the form of physical construction.

Typically, though, the document or documents that specify an unbuilt architectural work turn out to be incomplete and internally inconsistent. In the extreme, there may be nothing more to go on than a few vague sketches. Even when unbuilt designs are highly developed and documented, they may not specify complete and consistent three-dimensional constructions; openings in plan may not line up with openings in elevation, columns may shift location from floor to floor, and so on. That abandoned projects should have this character is hardly surprising; designing is, after all, largely a process of developing details and of identifying and resolving problems and inconsistencies as this development takes place. Furthermore, it is commonplace to pursue multiple alternatives in parallel, and to resolve them into a unified proposition only at a fairly late stage.

But that is only the beginning of the difficulty; counterfactuals, in general, are very slippery things. They are only of real interest if the counterfactual premise specifies an apparently plausible alternative at some particular juncture in history. We might well, for example, be interested in counterfactual speculations that begin "If Le Corbusier had won the League of Nations competition" or "If Louis Kahn had happened to live a few years longer," but the premise "If Hitler and Mussolini had won the war" seems more problematic—and the architectural implications of the counterfactual premise "If the young Frank Lloyd Wright had played with Legos instead of Froebel blocks" seems too tenuous to be worth exploring. Some historians, indeed, have strongly argued the position that all counterfactual premises are meaningless and that exploring their consequences is simply a waste of time.

Furthermore, one cannot know for sure what would have followed if the counterfactual premise had been true. After all, many things could have turned out to influence or determine what happened subsequently—perhaps in surprising ways. At best one can develop a reasonably consistent and plausible account, based on necessarily imperfect knowledge of these factors, of what might have followed.

In the particular case of computer-generated architectural counterfactuals, we are asked to accept a string of premises: "If the architect had completed the design, and if the building had then been constructed, and if it had been photographed from a particular viewpoint, then you would have seen this." If we are prepared to suspend disbelief to this extent, we must then consider whether the author of the reconstruction has convincingly spun out the consequences. Has the design been completed in a plausible and satisfying way, as the original architect might have done so? (And how can we ever know?) Has missing information been appropriately filled in, and have ambiguities and inconsistencies been resolved in acceptable fashion? Has knowledge of relevant construction processes and conditions been effectively applied in describing surfaces and details?

Frequently, computer-generated images of unbuilt buildings are electronically merged with current photographs of their sites. These hybrids present the architectural counterfactual in its most dramatic and provocative form. They claim, in effect: "Here is what this place might have been." Perhaps. But we can never know for sure.

Predictions

Yet other computer-generated images serve as predictions. Their authors claim, "If the given design is executed, then the result will look just like this." Sometimes such images are made in order to study design alternatives, and at other times their purpose is to show clients what they can expect to get. In any case, construction will ultimately show the accuracy or otherwise of predictive images, and the consequences of inaccurate prediction may be severe. Bad predictions may lead to bad decisions and attendant recriminations.

In this case, unlike the others we have considered so far, assuring the accuracy of the underlying 3D model is not the key scholarly issue. Here the model is simply a postulate, an intellectual construction that might well have been otherwise. The simulator's task is to combine the essentially arbitrary facts of the design with relevant facts and rules about the physical world, then accurately derive the visual consequences.

The physically based simulation algorithms that are used to produce such predictive images, and the parameters that control the execution of these algorithms, attempt to encode these facts and rules as accurately as possible. Then, execution of the computation applies them to derive scientifically defensible photo-realistic images. Thus, for example, popular software based on raytracing and radiosity principles is ultimately grounded on fundamental scientific laws of light reflection, transmission, and absorption. When the geometry and surface properties of a scene are accurately specified, together with the spatial and spectral distribution of energy from light sources, these algorithms compute distributions of light energy across surfaces. Because light interreflections within a scene may be complex, the necessary computations are often lengthy.

Surface intensities cannot directly be translated into a photorealistic display, however, because the intensity range of a scene is usually very much greater than the range that can be rendered by a given display or printing technique. (This is also the case, of course, with paintings and photographs.) So the wide computed intensity range must be compressed into the narrower one available on the chosen output device. A reasonable way to perform this task is to try to match the characteristics of photographic film as closely as possible so that the visible result may be regarded as a pseudophotograph made by a virtual camera. Then, once the building has been constructed, the predictive image may be compared directly with a photograph taken from the same spot and under the same lighting conditions.

Judgments

Although the images in this book share many technical and visual characteristics, they turn out to serve a wide variety of purposes. Computer-generated architectural reconstructions show us what was, reports depict what is, counterfactuals speculate about what might have been, and predictions attempt to illustrate what will be. The production processes differ correspondingly, and so do the standards of scholarly judgment; we expect reconstructions to be informed by historical knowledge and sound scholarly judgment, we want reports to be careful and honest, we require counterfactuals to be plausible and intellectually stimulating, and we look to predictions to provide reliable guidance for our future actions.

William J. Mitchell
Dean, School of Architecture
Massachusetts Institute of Technology

Introduction

Computer graphics technology is proving invaluable to practicing architects and their clients for visualizing a design before it is built. But digital imagery is also being developed for some buildings without any intention of their actually being constructed. This book explores the variety of reasons architects pursue the digital unbuilt.

- *To help archaeologists visualize the original state of their excavations*
- *To teach the lay public about archaeology and architectural history*
- *To practice the art and craft of architectural design*
- *To teach architecture students about great buildings*
  —even if they were never actually built
- *To study the changes in urban patterns through time*
- *To resurrect work of a famous architect whose work was unfortunately destroyed*
- *To provide a realistic backdrop for a retelling of a culture's history*
- *To teach children about space exploration*

The list goes on, with nearly as many reasons as models. If there is a common thread among all these projects, it is the testament they make to the skill and imagination of the contributors. Whether you are interested in traveling to a past that no longer exists or to a future that will never be, you can immerse yourself in an imaginary environment that is both credible and exciting.

Another key characteristic of many of these projects is the extent to which they depend on collaboration among professionals from differing fields. Architects, archaeologists, art historians, and computer scientists have all shown their handiwork here, yet any one group in isolation would probably be unable to accomplish this. It is only through working together, with each group adding its unique viewpoint and knowledge, that the collaborations can exist. For example, architects are accustomed to working with three-dimensional visualizations; archaeologists work more often with 2D sketches. When the two groups work together, archaeologists can see reconstructed buildings more clearly and detect areas where information is missing. Their subsequent work of filling in the missing data both improves the model and informs the archaeological study.

How Models Are Made

Modeling 3D objects on a computer can be compared to building a scale model from children's blocks and clay. Simple forms, such as cubes, spheres, and cylinders, which are programmed into the computer, can be grouped together and positioned like wooden blocks. Like clay, they can be resized and reshaped, usually with the aid of a hand-held mouse. Complex forms, such as buildings and cities, involve hundreds or thousands of such manipulations. When the model's form is complete, the modeler can add life to its appearance by assigning each piece a color or texture and specifying the type and location of lighting. Then the computer computes a rendering: by combining information about color, light, and shapes, it calculates the light color and intensity of every point on the screen. Depending on the complexity of the model and the power of the machine, such rendering can take a few minutes or many hours. After a rendering is computed and saved, it can be further manipulated with image-processing software. Thousands of such renderings displayed in rapid succession make an animation. Recent developments in computer technology have provided shortcuts for creating traditionally time-consuming animations. The viewer, by moving the computer's mouse, can walk through a model in real time or view a prepared 360-degree panorama of the scene. The CD-ROM that accompanies this book demonstrates several forms of such multimedia, providing a dynamic view of many of the projects illustrated in the book with still images.

The software used to create this work ranges from simple 2D drawing programs to the most sophisticated professional architectural computer-aided design (CAD) software. It is all listed in Appendix B. Many of the contributors to the book have additional projects on their World Wide Web sites. Those are listed, along with contact and credit information, in Appendix A.

Part I:
Reconstructing Lost Buildings

Numerous examples of historic buildings have been physically destroyed but electronically recreated. Architects and archaeologists, often working with sketchy data, have reconstructed not only ancient buildings but whole towns. They base their work on aging blueprints, ancient writings, and/or archaeological digs, and produce detailed, credible constructions. The resulting 3D models provide both stunning imagery and important insights into our architectural history and our ancestors' sense of space.

The Northwest Palace of Ashur-nasir-pal at Nimrud, Assyria is an example of a reconstruction in process—a very unusual process. The image shown is the compilation of historic and visual imagery collected from all over the world. The palace was built between 900 and 800 B.C. and excavated in the 1840s. Since then, many of its artifacts have been sold to museums and collectors all over the United States, Europe, and Asia. It would be impossible now to reassemble all these components in one place. Instead, the researchers are collecting photographs of the dispersed objects and combining them with the *in situ* remains of the palace—now a museum—as re-excavated and restored by the British, Poles, and Iraqis since the 1950s.

The modelers scan these photos into a computer and apply the images as texture maps onto the various surfaces of a 3D model. The result is a startlingly realistic picture of what the architecture and decoration of the palace might have looked like nearly three millennia ago. The research is being carried out by archaeologist Samuel M. Paley of the State University of New

A preliminary image of the Northwest Palace of Ashur-nasir-pal at Nimrud, Assyria, features photographs of real artifacts superimposed on the 3D model. Research is ongoing, conducted by Samuel M. Paley, Richard P. Sobolewski, and Alison B. Snyder, with modeling by Learning Sites, Inc.

Frank Lloyd Wright's Pauson house was built in 1938 near Phoenix, Arizona, for sisters Rose and Gertrude Pauson. Constructed from local materials, it stood for only a few years before being destroyed by fire. The house was modeled and rendered by Asli Suner, an architecture student at the University of Southern California.

York at Buffalo, architect Richard P. Sobolewski of Warsaw, Poland, and architect Alison B. Snyder of the University of Oregon. The modeling is being conducted by Learning Sites, Inc. When it is completed, around 2000, the interactive model will be a living museum of the palace. Viewers will be able to "walk" through the simulated space, select artifacts to examine more closely, and peruse a database of visual, cultural, and historic information about it.

It is not only ancient buildings that have been lost. Some recent architectural masterpieces have also been destroyed, many in war or fire, but some through deliberate demolition. In the name of historic preservation, society now usually goes to great lengths to save any structure by great architects. This has not always been the case. For example, the famous American architect Frank Lloyd Wright was not always as revered as he is today. Earlier in this century, some of his works were recklessly destroyed, but now some of them have been resurrected as computer models.

A Caveat

Although most of the images in this book look very polished and professional, it is unwise to accept them as absolute truth. In most cases, the modelers of destroyed buildings work with incomplete information and must make assumptions and educated guesses to fill in the gaps. In some cases the unknown is made clear: portions of a model may be uncolored or undetailed, for example. In other cases it's impossible to tell what was documented and what was guesswork.

Professional architects, archaeologists, and historians should apply the same healthy skepticism to these images as they would to any other visualization produced from scant data. Amateurs interested in experiencing another time and culture should feel free to explore these spaces—but remain aware that what they see on the page is not necessarily historically precise.

Classical Theaters: Still Playing to Modern Audiences

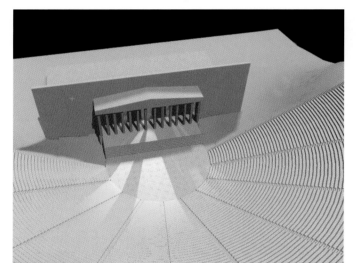

Just as ancient Greek drama has profoundly influenced Western literature, so have the classical theaters where those dramas were performed influenced centuries of Western architecture. Greek tragedies of the fifth century B.C. were based on mythology or history and were laden with religious, moral, or political messages. They were performed in open-air theaters that were often cut into hillsides. The sloped seating meant better views and acoustics for the audience. The stage was typically circular, and behind it was a building, called a *skene*, for use by the actors. These theaters, when viewed in plan, reveal a strong geometric structure.

At the University of British Columbia in Vancouver, Canada, Professor Jerzy Wojtowicz asked his students to model examples of theaters long since destroyed or ruined. Examples shown here are from Greece, Eritrea, and Rome. These exercises serve both as a vehicle for learning computer techniques and as a medium for studying the classical forms. When rendered with realistic lighting for both daytime and nighttime performances, the theaters show off a beautiful ambience that must have inspired ancient audiences to contemplate the cosmos. The students created plan and cross-section line drawings of their chosen theater in MiniCad and modeled it in form·Z; then they rendered selected views with Wavefront Advanced Visualizer.

Reconstruction of a classical Greek theater, modeled by Robert Fabianiak.

Paraskenion theater by Glen Stokes,
in which the parascenia are two wings
that extend forward from the skene.

Theater of Eritrea,
modeled by Agata Malczyk.

Theater of Eritrea,
modeled by Agata Malczyk.

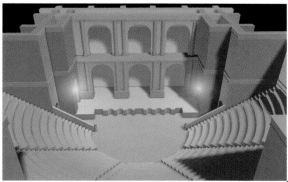

A reconstruction of the Late Roman
Odeum at Buthrotum, modeled by
Murray Gilmour.

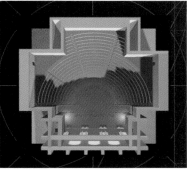

As compelling as many of these computer graphics images are, they are seldom constructed for their own sake. In the case of the ancient Greek Vari House, which now exists only as fragmentary excavated stone walls, the goal is primarily educational.

The Vari House:
Ancient Beekeepers
Teach Budding Archaeologists

This farmhouse, which is believed to have been occupied around 325–275 B.C., was constructed by Learning Sites, Inc., a company motivated by the educational potential of real archaeological sites. Architect-trained archaeologist Donald Sanders and his colleagues have carefully researched the sites, created 3D models of the buildings, artifacts, and surroundings, and woven them together into a multimedia package that can be tailored for such diverse groups as schoolchildren, adult museum-goers, and fellow archaeologists.

Key to the multimedia experience is the virtual reality modeling language, or VRML. VRML models can be navigated by moving and clicking a mouse or joystick. Users can "walk" through the 3D environment, examine artifacts they find, and call up textual, graphic, and audible information about what they see. The Learning Sites environments include a strong pedagogical component: students are given background information about what they find, and then are asked to draw conclusions from the archaeological evidence. In short, they experience the continuous questioning that a real archaeologist might go through in determining the age, purpose, materials, and other pertinent information about a structure. For example, thick walls are shown to be bearing walls, while thinner partitions do not carry additional loads. The thickest walls of the Vari House were believed to support a two-story tower. Clues such as this enabled the researchers to draw conclusions about the three-dimensional appearance of the structure.

A Greek farmhouse, believed to have been occupied around 325–275 B.C. near the ancient town of Vari, was reconstructed by Learning Sites, Inc. Principal Donald Sanders and his colleagues built a model in the Virtual Reality Modeling Language (VRML) with information from a 1960s excavation by British archaeologists.

Archaeologists have concluded that the unusual pots they found were bee skeps, designed to encourage honeybees to build comb inside and to enable people to remove the honey easily.

Interacting with the VRML model, a user can navigate at will and approach the Vari House. As one comes closer, the structural detail becomes more clear, as does the main entry.

Here, for example, is a set of questions that might help students arrive at their own conclusion about the purpose of a row of circular stones with central depressions. They had already learned that colonnades were common in ancient Greece because open structures provided shade from the sun but let in the cooling breezes.

What do you think the circular stones with the central depression were used for? (Look at their spacing and size.)

How would archaeologists go about reconstructing their use?

What features of other ancient Greek buildings would help you determine the use of these objects?

One of the mysteries that the real archaeologists had to solve, which the students are also asked to ponder, is the occupation of the Vari House inhabitants. Unusually shaped pot fragments were found at the site. The region was renowned in Aristotle's day for producing the best honey in the Greek world. These clues, together with chemical evidence of honey traces found inside the fragments

and awareness of similar pots seen in ancient Egyptian art depicting honey production, led archaeologists to conclude the Vari House was occupied by a family of beekeepers. This guided process of discovery not only helps students appreciate the culture of the original inhabitants and understand their architectural environment but also stimulates the students' creative problem solving and may even inspire some to become archaeologists.

These multimedia productions are the collaborative work of many disciplines. Eventually, principal Sanders believes, architects, archaeologists, artists, engineers, educators, computer technicians, software designers, and telecommunications experts will be working together to create entire libraries of such interactive virtual environments. So far, Learning Sites has produced a variety of re-creations of buildings and sites in Egypt, Turkey, Greece, and the Sudan.

Moving through the main central space of the building, one sees dirt floors and stone slab paving. Glimpses through open doors encourage exploration.

As the student explorer enters the northwest room, more clues about beekeeping practices and the age of the structure are revealed.

The excavated and reconstructed house is furnished with artifacts, such as pots and bee skeps, that provide links within VRML to further information about the structure, its inhabitants, and their occupation.

The Vari House had four rooms across the back of the building, a large central space, and two spaces in the front corners. Each room had only one doorway, which opened to the central space. The excavators found no shelters for keeping large animals and no grain storage facilities. This supported their conclusion that the inhabitants were beekeepers.

Because one important purpose of the Vari House model is to lead schoolchildren through a realistic archaeological inquiry, the site is furnished with artifacts, clues, and textual questions throughout.

Reconstructing an archaeological ruin as a computer model often requires a good deal of detective work to determine how the building may have appeared in its prime. It also involves educated guesswork. No wonder, then, that one use for such models is an environment for a mystery-solving computer game.

The Mausoleum of Qin:
The Game of Archaeology

Mieczyslaw Boryslawski and France Israel of the San Francisco multimedia firm View by View, Inc., created a model of the tomb of the Chinese Emperor Qin Shihuangdi. Learn Technologies Interactive has incorporated it into the CD-ROM–based educational game "Qin: Tomb of the Middle Kingdom," published by Time Warner. People playing the game learn about Chinese culture and history as they navigate the recreated spaces. Their learning reflects, to some extent, that which is experienced by the researchers and modelers in their recreation process.

The Alchemy Chamber. The as-yet unexcavated tomb of the Chinese emperor Qin Shihuangdi has come alive in the computer game "Qin: Tomb of the Middle Kingdom," by Learn Technologies Interactive. The chambers of the tomb were modeled and rendered by View by View, Inc., based on their knowledge of Chinese architecture and artifacts of the time.

In the second century B.C., the young King Zheng came to power in the small kingdom of Qin, in the city of Xi'an, an important trading center and provincial capital of Shaanxi in east central China. By 221 B.C. he had conquered his neighbors, unified China for the first time, and declared himself emperor Qin Shihuangdi. The ruthless leader drafted hundreds of thousands of workers and artisans to build a huge mausoleum for his eventual burial. As was the practice in ancient China for the rich and powerful, the tomb was outfitted with all the comforts of life, including food, household items, and servants who were sacrificed and possibly buried alive. The mausoleum's construction took nearly forty years. Qin Shihuangdi also put people to work connecting existing portions of the Great Wall of China and building thousands of miles of roads and canals. His centralized administrative institutions that helped to unite the new empire endured for over 2000 years. In spite of these accomplishments, he was feared and hated. He burned books, sentenced Confucian scholars to death who opposed him, and sacrificed countless workers and soldiers throughout his lifetime. Shortly after his death in 207 B.C.,

The Dining Chamber and Emperor's Chamber of the unexcavated tomb.

a popular rebellion ended his dynasty and destroyed and buried much of the tomb and surrounding structures.

In 1974, Chinese archaeologists uncovered buried terra-cotta statues near the tomb site. Dubbed the eighth wonder of the world, this find was eventually discovered to be a life-size army of about 6000 handcrafted soldiers and horses, which Qin Shihuangdi had ordered made to guard his tomb. These remarkably preserved figures, along with bronze swords, spears, and crossbows, have now been largely excavated and are visited by millions of tourists every year. Fragments of surviving paint enabled restorers to repaint them in their original bright colors.

However, the tomb these terra-cotta soldiers guard has not yet been excavated, though some of it is believed to remain intact, and this task

may take decades. How then to model the tomb itself? "We made a lot of educated guesses," says View by View vice president France Israel, "to model what archaeologists might find when they finally get there. We drew on investigations done at Harvard University and in China. We know what neighboring architecture of the period was like and have based our own imagery on that."

The View by View team developed their model with form·Z software and rendered it in Electric Image, with material textures scanned from photographs of real artifacts and buildings of the period. They had no dimensioned drawings to work from and relied instead on sketches, drawings, photographs, and intuition. In the game, players take the role of amateur archaeologists

who interpret the artifacts they find as they navigate the labyrinthine rooms. In the process, they learn about Chinese culture while coming to appreciate the elaborate and beautifully furnished home-after-death of the former emperor. Boryslawski believes one reason the game is exciting is that players can excavate the tomb before archaeologists do.

The first Chinese emperor, Qin Shihuangdi, is presumed to lie in peace in his unexcavated tomb. The richly adorned chamber is filled with treasures to accompany the emperor into the afterlife. After his death, the entire tomb was covered and landscaped. The resulting mound resembled a mountain, lessening its appeal to grave robbers.

The music chamber and library. Chinese emperors were sent to their grave with all the comforts of home, including furnishings, household items, and servants. In the computer game, players learn about Chinese culture while examining the artifacts in each chamber.

The emperor's burial chamber was filled with rich treasures and, to discourage thieves, rivers of mercury were cut into the floors.

Although the mausoleum itself has not yet been excavated, archaeologists have unearthed thousands of life-size terra-cotta soldiers that were lined up to guard the emperor in death. These statues have been remarkably preserved.

Among the many reasons architects choose to create 3D models, perhaps the most compelling is the quest to further human knowledge in seemingly unrelated fields. One such project

Ceren: A Village Rediscovered

occurred at the University of Colorado, where architecture students' modeling aided anthropologists in unraveling some mysteries of a Central American village destroyed by volcanic ash some fourteen centuries ago.

Structure 7 in Ceren demonstrates the pattern of light and shadow created by the door. Some pots are suspended from the roof beams to conserve space.

It was probably approaching dusk in the pre-Columbian village of Ceren in what is now western El Salvador. When tremors alerted the villagers to the impending disaster, they had no time to collect their belongings before fleeing. What happened to the villagers is unknown; what happened to their village has been the subject of intense study by anthropologists for over twenty years. The volcanic ash that rained down on the village helped to preserve the structures and their contents. The many household items that were left behind have given anthropologists a field day in interpreting the daily lives of ordinary people.

Much of the archaeological research conducted in this region centers on the large temple-pyramids and other structures inhabited by the elite of the pre-Columbian cultures. In Ceren, by contrast, the remains show evidence of modest thatched huts equipped with a variety of ceramic pots, stone axes, and other utilitarian household items. A study of these artifacts and their placement within the structures tells researchers volumes about the domestic activities of the rural villagers. By studying the amount of ash found under the ceramic shards, archaeologists can determine whether a pot was on the ground before the eruption or whether it fell when the roof collapsed after a considerable amount of ashfall. They have been able to surmise that the pots were stored at various heights within the huts. Some were suspended from roof beams, some placed on wall tops or shelves.

This 360-degree panorama of Structure 6 was created as input to an interactive animation. The evident distortion disappears in the animation, in which a computer user can navigate simply by dragging the mouse.

But the archaeological data, in raw form, did not communicate this very well. Artifact location is normally recorded through a combination of floor plans, textual descriptions, and tabular data to indicate the third dimension, height. However, these separate data forms are difficult to interpret as a whole. To bring these plans and tables to life, anthropologist Scott Simmons called on Jenniffer Lewin and other architecture students at the University of Colorado's Sundance Laboratory to plug the data into 3D modeling software so he could study the resulting images. This was easier said than done. When engaged in the exacting work of creating the models, Lewin discovered many inconsistencies in the data that were not apparent from the plans and tables. Such inconsistencies were the understandable consequence of combining the field notes of many people with diverse professional interests working over the two decades of excavation. So Lewin, Simmons, and the rest of the team worked closely together to reinterpret the data, in many cases going back to the original excavation notes.

Resolving these inconsistencies led to unexpected results. For example, to explain discrepancies between wall and column heights, the researchers concluded that the structures probably had horizontal openings that were not readily apparent from archaeologists' drawings and notes. From the older drawings, one might have concluded that the huts' interiors were fairly dark and airless. By orienting the structures properly and applying computed sun angles, the students were able to create displays that show how direct sunlight and indirect light entered the huts at various times of day.

The students studied photographs and consulted researchers who had been to the site to determine appropriate colors and material textures. The resulting images show the play of light and the distribution of realistic-looking artifacts that turn a collection of dry data into a lively stage set for real-life drama. Simmons credits the visual textures and the visible relationship between artifacts for aiding his interpretations. He says, "the powerful thing these renderings have done is to help us understand more clearly how people organized and used household activity spaces, storage spaces, and work spaces around the buildings. The images show relationships of artifacts to different areas of the building that's hard to see when your drawings show only broken pot shards on the floor of the structure."

The students modeled and rendered the structures and artifacts with form·Z modeling software on Macintosh computers.

Structure 2 in the excavated village of Ceren shows a detail of the hut's walls and roof, with spacing in between for light. Pots were stored on the wall tops; some were hidden below a shelf. The computer model better enables anthropologists to understand the domestic life of this ancient people by illustrating the way they used their household and storage spaces.

The sweat bath of Ceren is dubbed Structure 9. Here, the thatch roof and dome are exposed for a view down to the fire pit.

The interior of Ceren's Structure 12 shows typical materials and the open space above the columns and wall.

A view of structure 11 shows a shelf and raised artifacts.

The interior of Structure 3 shows the door and roof detail.

The walls of Structure 6 were being rebuilt during the time of the eruption that destroyed the village.

Structure 1 shows the window openings at the corners, a detail that had been poorly understood before this model was built. Note the hanging chili peppers, which survived thanks to the preservative properties of the volcanic ash.

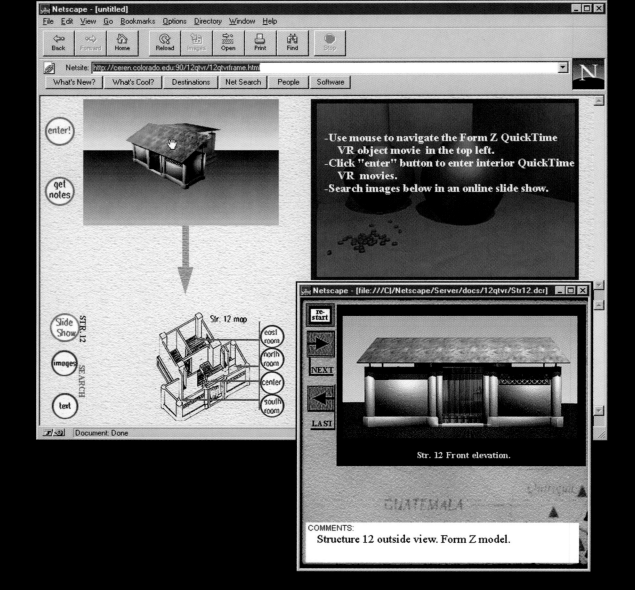

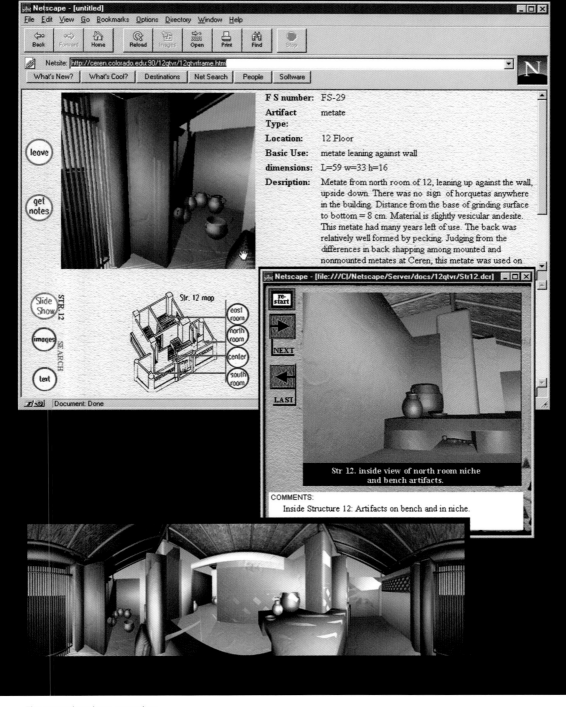

The researchers have created an educational World Wide Web site that offers available information about the Ceren excavation. Above left is an interior animation. The user has selected the metate artifact, and information about it is displayed to the right. Below right is an image from a "slide show" and at the bottom is the 360-degree panorama of Structure 12.

One of the most intriguing mysteries in North American archaeology lies in what is now the southwestern United States. It was here, beginning around A.D. 500, that the Anasazi people flourished. They were master architects, farmers, potters, and jewelers, who left behind traces of these arts at Mesa Verde in southwestern Colorado, at Chaco Canyon in northwestern New Mexico, and throughout the surrounding region. Much of their culture has been passed down to their descendants, the contemporary Pueblo people. However, around 1150 the Anasazi who lived in Chaco Canyon abandoned their homes and mysteriously disappeared.

The Chetro Ketl Great Kiva:
The Center of the Anasazi Universe

What they left behind has been the focus of archaeological curiosity for over a century. The Chetro Ketl site in Chaco Canyon is the special interest of archaeologist John Kantner of the University of California at Santa Barbara. The Great House, one of several located in the canyon, is a four-story, 337-room masonry structure that probably marked an important center for trade, government, and religion for the Anasazi. Kantner has particularly focused on the ruins of the Great Kivas, which are large underground ceremonial pits. He combined the excavated physical evidence with cultural assumptions from surviving traditions and developed a computer model of how the kivas must have looked to their inhabitants a millennium ago.

The Chetro Ketl Great Kiva, as excavated and modeled, is about 18 meters (59 feet) in diameter, and its floor may have been up to 5 meters (over 16 feet) below ground level. A low masonry bench skirts the perimeter and near the center is a hollow rectangular firebox. The entrance was probably through an adjacent antechamber or though a hole in the roof and down a ladder. The walls display a collection of symbolic art and house irregularly spaced crypts, where intact and valuable treasures were found by twentieth-century archaeologists. This dark and smoky environment is probably the place where feasting and religious ritual took place.

One of the most remarkable features of the Great Kiva was its roof. Though little of the wood survives, its existence is surmised by four large masonry wells in the floor that probably

The roof was one of the most remarkable aspects of this underground structure. Twenty large beams and perhaps many of the 900 smaller ones had to be imported from forests many miles away.

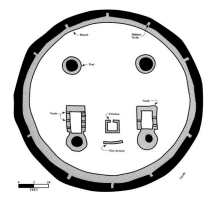

The floor plan of the Chetro Ketl Great Kiva in New Mexico shows the relationship between the four massive posts, the central firebox, the surrounding bench, and the irregularly spaced niches that hid valuable treasure.

served as foundations for the huge structural posts that supported the roof. One remaining post fragment is 66 centimeters (26 inches) in diameter. The surrounding forests of piñon and juniper would not have produced trees large or straight enough to serve as these posts, so archaeologists believe that timber must have been imported from spruce forests as far away as 60 kilometers, or nearly 40 miles. It has been estimated that 200,000 beams may have been required to roof all of the canyon's structures. This further reinforces the probable importance of Chetro Ketl as a regional center and may partly explain why the Anasazi built such an impressive network of roads. The roof configuration in the model is patterned after some better-preserved ones elsewhere in New Mexico. It includes twenty large beams and 900 smaller ones. The larger beams are darker in color, indicating that, being particularly valuable, they may have been reused many times.

Except for the smoke hole in the roof, there would have been few places for daylight to penetrate the kiva. The dark interior may have contributed to the surreal atmosphere of the ceremonies performed there. As Kantner says, "The flickering light would certainly have augmented the mystery and supernatural aura of the ceremonial events occurring in the kiva, illuminating the masked dancers and casting unnatural shadows on the walls."

Artifacts found in the Great Kiva further inform us about the life of the Anasazi people and of the rituals that may have taken place there. The great variety of pottery supports the theory that this was a center of pilgrimage to which pots and their contents of food and valuables were imported from surrounding regions. The hidden, plaster-covered wall crypts contained necklaces that were from 200 to 500 centimeters (7 to 17 feet) in length, each containing from 1000 to 2000 stone and shell beads and turquoise pendants, crafted by master jewelers.

In most excavations, such crypts were long since emptied, perhaps robbed, so this find was particularly valuable. The treasure was possibly hidden because the beads and pendants held sacred significance or high monetary value.

In the actual excavation of Chetro Ketl no murals were found, but Kantner added some to his model based on art inscribed in the rock walls of similar excavations in the region. The exact symbolic meaning of the rock art will of course never be known, but archaeologists can make educated guesses based on the role of familiar symbols in the lives of today's Pueblo people. For example, hand prints may have signified signatures of supplicants; turkeys may have symbolized the earth, springs, streams, and mountains, which are the homes of the cloud spirits. The spiral, an abstract art form found all over the world, may have represented the journey of the people in search of Tuwanasavi, the center of the universe. The flute player Kokopelli may have represented fertility and lizards may represent ancestors. Abstract designs, like those found in pottery and textiles, may have been used to designate local group affiliations, or they may have served simply as decoration. Whatever the meaning of these graphic representations, they contributed to the ambience of these ceremonial spaces that must have been enormously important in the lives of the Anasazi people.

John Kantner modeled the Chetro Ketl Great Kiva on a Macintosh computer with Specular Infini-D software.

A ladder leading up to the smoke hole
may have been the only way in and
out of this underground structure.

Artifacts found in the excavated kiva may have come from many miles away, reinforcing the idea that Chetro Ketl may have been an important regional center for trade, government, and religion for the Anasazi people.

In the Chetro Ketl Great Kiva, the fire would have been the only light source. The dark and smoky atmosphere probably contributed to the mystery the ceremonies held here, as did the art painted on the circular walls; its symbolic significance can only be guessed at today.

Exactly how the Anasazi people used and felt about their kivas we may never know. But judging from the elaborate structures and art work, we can guess that these kivas held ceremonies at the very core of the Anasazi spirituality.

It is difficult to recreate a lost structure from scant archaeological remains, but when that structure underwent many transformations throughout its history, it is more difficult still to present a clear picture of how it looked at various stages. The Cathedral of Florence, Italy, had several incarnations from its first erection around A.D. 500 to its sixteenth-century reconstruction.

Santa Reparata, Santa Maria Del Fiore:
The Evolution of a Cathedral

Sorting through the evidence of remaining foundations, historic writings, and early drawings has been the work of a multidisciplinary team led by architectural historian Christine Smith and architect George Liaropoulos-Legendre, both professors at Harvard University. They have researched and modeled a series of computer recreations that show the church in both form and function and used that medium to demonstrate the structure's changes over time. In some cases, firm historical evidence is unavailable or inconsistent, and they have had to rely on their general knowledge of the architecture of the era. The resulting images are deliberately abstract so as not to imply a greater precision than the researchers have complete confidence in.

The first set of images represents a best guess about the appearance of the early Christian church of Santa Reparata, believed to have been built in the fifth or sixth century on the foundations of a Roman house and workshop in Florence. The basilica was long and rectangular in plan. The nave, or principal part of the interior, was flanked by two side aisles and separated from them by a row of columns. Wooden trusses spanned the high nave roof; the aisles had lower roofs above which high clerestory windows provided illumination. A vaulted apse protruded at the east end, making a backdrop for the altar.

In its first incarnation, the Cathedral of Florence was an early Christian basilica, with a rectangular nave flanked by two side aisles. Harvard University professors Christine Smith and George Liaropoulos-Legendre and their students modeled the church Santa Reparata as it changed through the ages.

Around 1050, as shown in the second set of images, a Romanesque church replaced the early Christian basilica. The colonnade was replaced by seven piers. The choir, the space between the nave and the apse, was raised, and below it were vaulted crypts. Stairs led up to the choir from the ends of the two side aisles.

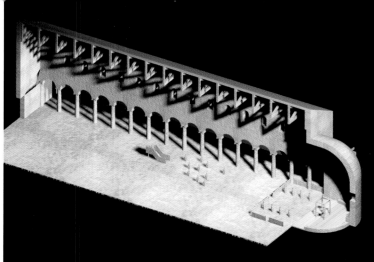

The third set of images show the transition that occurred, as Smith hypothesizes, between 1358 and 1436. As the much larger cathedral of Santa Maria del Fiore was built, the older Romanesque church was gradually demolished. The surreal quality of the images suggests the gradual emergence of one and disappearance of the other. The old walls and roof remained standing as the new structure was built around them. Then the walls were removed, but the choir remained standing and functioned as the high altar area in the new cathedral. Finally, the apse wall was removed and the high vaults of the new structure completed. The net effect of this sequence is a visual illustration of historical building patterns through time.

Liaropoulos-Legendre and his students used AutoCAD and Alias Wavefront to model the buildings, Adobe Photoshop to further develop still images of selected views, and Macromedia Director to integrate all the material in CD-ROM form.

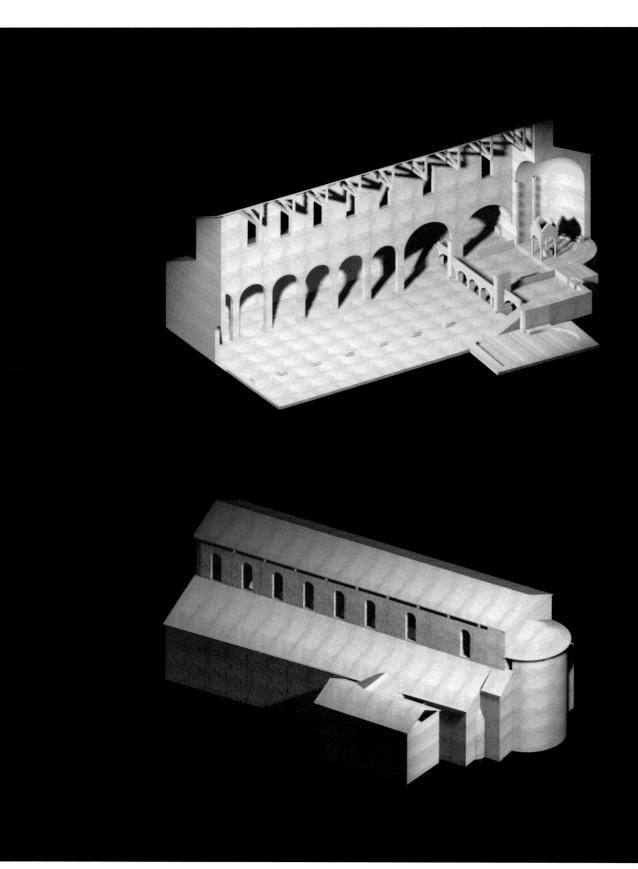

In its final form, in the fourteenth and fifteenth centuries, remnants of the older churches were gradually removed as the new cathedral of Santa Maria del Fiore was built around them.

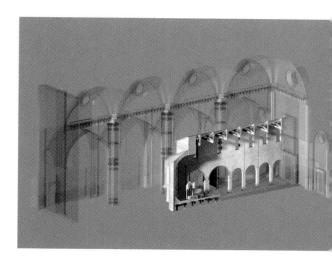

In the eleventh century, a Romanesque church replaced the early Christian basilica. Seven piers replaced the colonnade, and the choir was raised.

For over a thousand years, the city of Cairo, Egypt, has been growing and transforming. It began as a geometrically simple plan in the mind of its founder, the tenth-century Caliph al-Mu'izz, and is now a complicated, crowded, bustling metropolis. How did those changes occur over the years? What was the urban experience of its inhabitants at transitional points in the city's development? These are some of the questions that challenge architectural historian Nezar AlSayyad and his colleagues at the University of California at Berkeley.

Cairo: A City in Flux through Time

To understand the evolution of Cairo, AlSayyad, Yehuda Kalay, and Ame Eliot developed a collection of computer models that simulate the city at three key periods in its history (A.D. 969, 1169, and 1517). By piecing together carefully researched data from maps, photographs, archaeological evidence, and the writings and drawings of pre-twentieth-century travelers, these researchers have created a "four-dimensional" picture of the medieval city through models that describe the city at varying levels of abstraction.

In the tenth century, Egypt was conquered by the Shiite Fatimid clan, and Caliph al-Mu'izz ordered that a new walled city be built to house his caliphate and his army. A site on the Nile River was laid out in a fairly regular geometry. It featured a hierarchical placement of monumental palaces and mosques, wide streets, formal gardens, and, in the middle, a public square capable of holding 10,000 soldiers in formation. It was named Al-Qahirah, "The City Victorious." Within the walls of this city, only the royalty and military were permitted to live. This was consistent with the Shiite belief in a royal Islam that keeps both church and state in the hands of the family of the prophet Mohammed. Merchants were allowed to bring their wares into the city by day, but they had to leave again every night. The city's grandeur and formality seem at odds with the irregular, organic forms more common to Islamic cities, and which, indeed, characterize present-day Cairo. What happened?

Nezar AlSayyad and his colleagues at the University of California at Berkeley modeled the ancient city of Cairo at three different points in its history. The original city, as designed in A.D. 969, was relatively simple, as seen in this clay massing model. A fly-over view of their computer model shows the city in 1169. By the year 1517 the huge open spaces had been filled in with shops and housing, making the streets narrower and more crowded.

As early as 1243, traveler Ibn Sa'id described Cairo as crowded and claustrophobic, filled with narrow, twisting, irregular streets and mud brick houses with little air or light. By then, the populist Sunni had taken over the city. AlSayyad attributes the change in urban character to a deliberate attempt by the succeeding Ayyubid dynasty to "erase the remnants of the Fatimid caliphate and facilitate the transformation of Egypt from a Shiite to a Sunni state." To win favor among the common folk, the Sunni permitted the merchants and the poor to move into the central city, where they built small shops and houses as infill in the monumental squares. Without central planning, which was instrumental at the city's founding, this organic growth turned the once broad streets into narrow, labyrinthine passages housing the vibrant activities of people at work and play. Further transformations occurred over the centuries as successive dynasties took power and initiated new building programs that were followed by periods of decay.

To dramatize the change—both architectural and social—AlSayyad began developing computer models of the city for the three time periods with whatever information he could find. Some portions of the city, such as surviving mosques, could be modeled in exquisite detail. An animation of a walk-through such a building gives the modern viewer a vivid picture of what such spaces were like. Other portions of the city had far less documentation and could be appreciated only within the context of massing models. These models were, when seen as a sequence through time and from a bird's-eye view, effective in showing the gradual infill of the large squares over time.

"Writing history," AlSayyad notes, "is an art of interpretation, not a science of representation. The stories we depict will change from time to time and place to place to reflect the interests of those who tell them. The challenge in using this medium in the telling of history will, perhaps, be in finding the proper balance."

AlSayyad and his colleagues built their models of Cairo on Silicon Graphics workstations with Alias and Softimage software. With funding from the National Endowment for the Arts, they created a half-hour documentary, including computer animations, for public television.

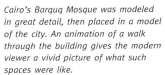
Cairo's Barquq Mosque was modeled
in great detail, then placed in a model
of the city. An animation of a walk
through the building gives the modern
viewer a vivid picture of what such
spaces were like.

To compile a detailed image of what
Cairo looked like in ancient times,
AlSayyad drew on a variety of sources.
A painting by nineteenth-century
British artist David Roberts, for exam-
ple, gives a dramatic rendering of
the entrance of the Qalawan complex.
Inaccuracies could be resolved by
comparing the drawing to a photo-
graph of the same structure.

In the mid-thirteenth century, Kublai Khan, fifth emperor of the Mongol Empire and grandson of Genghis Khan, conquered northern China, established the Yuan dynasty, and built a city in what is now central Beijing. Though descended from nomadic Mongolian warriors, Kublai adopted the Chinese culture and system of government.

A Mongolian Palace Rebuilt:
Traces of Kublai Khan

By the fourteenth century, Kublai Khan had died and Chinese rebels had replaced his rule with the Ming dynasty. The palace was razed; the Forbidden City, in the middle of present-day Beijing, was built in its place.

Today, Chinese scholars, architects, and archaeologists are piecing together evidence of what Kublai Khan's palace must have looked like. They work from historic writings and drawings; they make educated guesses about decorative details by studying similar, contemporary structures nearby that have survived.

These images were created as part of a documentary series about the Mongolian Empire made for Japanese public television by the design division of the Taisei Corporation, a leading Japanese architecture, engineering, and construction company. Based in Tokyo and over 100 years old, the Taisei Corporation has recently become well known for its exquisite computer graphics reproductions.

In the thirteenth century, the Palace of Kublai Khan was the center of Chinese trade and culture. The Taisei Corporation's design division modeled the now lost city and created an animation for Japanese public television.

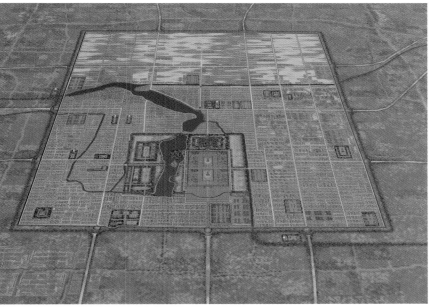

The formerly nomadic Mongolian warriors created a sophisticated walled city in what is now central Beijing.

The grounds of the Palace of Kublai Khan featured monumental gateways, formal gardens, and long, straight, broad avenues. The famous traveler Marco Polo returned to Europe with tales of his stay in this exotic city.

To determine detailing for the palace, Taisei modelers studied similar nearby structures that survived through the ages.

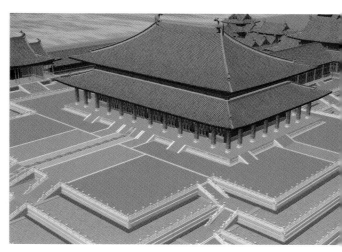

Founded in 1325, two hundred years before the Spanish conquistadors arrived, the city of Tenochtitlan was the center of the Aztec universe in what is now Mexico City. This bustling city of 200,000 inhabitants, one of the largest in the world at the time, was built on an island in Lake Texcoco and served as the political, cultural, and religious center of Aztec culture. In the middle of the city was Teocalli, the ceremonial precinct, where elaborate temples were built in alignment with celestial bodies.

Tenochtitlan: The Aztec Capital Restored to Life

It was here that frequent religious ceremonies took place, often concluding with human sacrifices to the gods. But when the conquering Hernán Cortés arrived in the early sixteenth century, he recognized the symbolic power the city provided the Aztecs and had it razed. He used the rubble to build his own city, symbolizing the new order, and over the ensuing centuries Tenochtitlan faded from memory. In accidental discoveries throughout the twentieth century, remains of the ancient city have been found, and gradually historians, archaeologists, and architects have been piecing together the evidence to reconstruct Teocalli.

One recent "rebuilder" is Antonieta Rivera, a Mexican architect now studying at the University of British Columbia in Canada. She has assembled information from the archaeological excavations and nearby surviving temples and from the writings and drawings of missionaries, conquistadors, and ancient Aztecs. Not surprisingly, these sources are not completely consistent with each other, but Rivera has been able to construct computer models of several interpretations of the data.

The Tiamatzincatl Temple is one of several temples of Teocalli reconstructed by Mexican architect Antonieta Rivera.

Central to her reconstruction is the geometry of archaeoastronomy. The Aztecs used the position of the sun at key times during the year to align their temples, calibrate their calendars, relate to the surrounding landscape, and thus stake a place for their culture in the universe. For example, the Templo Mayor, the most prominent structure in Teocalli, is aligned precisely

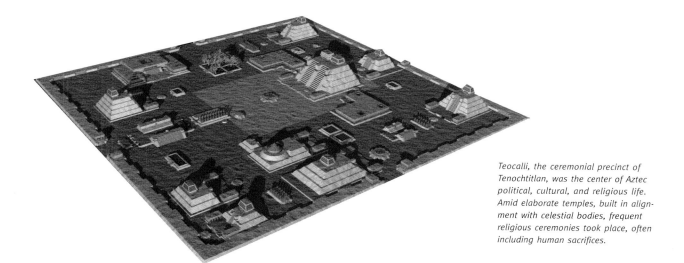

Teocalli, the ceremonial precinct of Tenochtitlan, was the center of Aztec political, cultural, and religious life. Amid elaborate temples, built in alignment with celestial bodies, frequent religious ceremonies took place, often including human sacrifices.

with the position of the sun at sunrise on the equinoxes (March 21 and September 21). This alignment and similar regulating lines helped Rivera determine not only the orientation but the shape, proportion, and location of the various temples. The digital nature of her models makes it easier to determine the relationships between the various structures and regulating lines than if she were using conventional clay models. Renderings of the models, as well as background information, are combined in an interactive CD-ROM that explains the culture and her discoveries.

As a testament to the scholarly importance of this work, Rivera was congratulated recently when she showed her work to archaeologist Eduardo Matos Moctezuma, director of Mexico City's Templo Mayor Museum. Although excavations of the ceremonial precinct have been going on for decades, no one had a complete and clear idea of the whole because so much of it is still covered by contemporary structures. Matos Moctezuma and his team were pleased to see a comprehensive view of the ceremonial precinct that they had never envisioned before. Further, they were astounded to see a structure only recently uncovered at the same location and orientation as Rivera had placed it based on her studies and interpretation. Arguably, the most important lesson this

illustrates is the potential power of an interdisciplinary approach to reconstructing archaeological sites. "Architects and archaeologists working together," Rivera concludes, "can make surprisingly accurate projections; this could be the first step into a new era in archaeological research."

Rivera modeled and animated Tenochtitlan on a Silicon Graphics workstation with Alias Wavefront. She then did her multimedia authoring and image, sound, and video processing on a Macintosh with Adobe Photoshop, SoundEdit, and Adobe Premiere.

The Templo Mayor of Tenochtitlan was at the heart of the ceremonial precinct. It is seen here from the ball court and from the ceremonial forest.

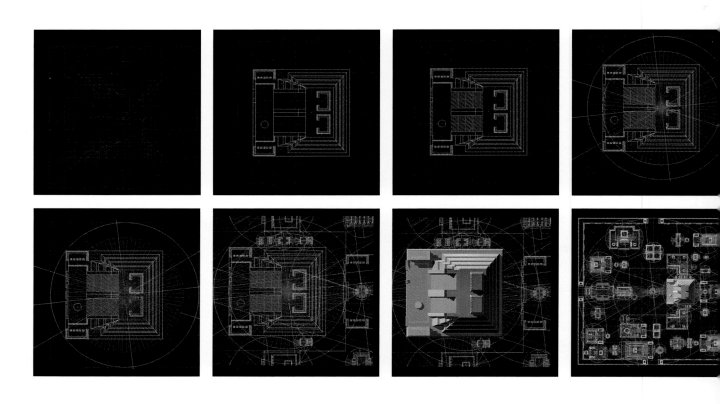

The skull rack of Teocalli was a grim reminder of the frequent human sacrifices to the Aztec gods.

The Ehecatl (Feathered Serpent) Temple as seen from the ceremonial bath of Teocalli.

In studying the relationship of the Templo Mayor, the Great Temple of Tenochtitlan, to the angular positions of the sun and stars, architect Antonieta Rivera drew a series of regulating lines. Her archaeoastronomical analysis revealed the alignment between these lines and various components of the temple.

Considering the high esteem Frank Lloyd Wright is now granted forty years after his death, it is nearly impossible to imagine the reasoning behind the tragic demolition of one of this country's earliest and finest contributions to modernist architecture. The Larkin Administration Building, completed in 1906 in Buffalo, New York, was remarkable in many respects, including its geometric massing, its use of then new technologies, and its clear expression of social ideals. Yet when it was demolished in 1950 for reasons related to the company's financial problems, scant documentation remained; the building was replaced by a parking lot.

The Larkin Building:
A Lost Monument to Modernism

The approach to the main door of the Larkin Building begins an animated walkthrough created by Kenneth Elwood to add a greater sense of space than still images can provide.

Rather than simply bemoan this loss, one researcher worked hard to reconstruct the Larkin Building in digital form. Kenneth Elwood, an architecture professor at the Savannah College of Art and Design in Georgia, spent four years in what he calls "post-demolition documentation." He painstakingly gathered what historic documentation —sketches, construction drawings, black-and-white photographs, writings—he could find, built a computer model of the entire building, and created an animation of a walk through the structure. To add a greater sense of realism and scale, he modeled the natural light in the original building, put furnishings in the central atrium and ancillary spaces, and simulated colors, textures, and materials throughout. Because the demolition process removed most of the building to a landfill, Elwood had to rely on diverse sources to determine its exact colors. He read firsthand descriptions written by Wright, his clients, and his critics. He even scraped beneath the surface of the infamous parking lot to find remaining samples of the exterior and interior brick.

The resulting video gives viewers a far more realistic impression of the building than they could possibly get from drawings and black-and-white photographs. These conventional media necessarily show only one view at a time and, because they are static, they place a layer of abstraction between the viewer and the building. The color and movement in Elwood's video bring a sense of reality and an appreciation of the building's complexity akin to actually experiencing the building directly. Sadly, it is the most direct experience most of us now living will ever know.

At the reception desk of the Larkin Building, looking back at the front entrance. As in many of his buildings, Wright also designed the furnishings and light fixtures.

When Wright was commissioned to design the Larkin Building shortly after the turn of the century, he was known primarily as a residential architect. This was to become his first important commercial design. Recognizing its importance to his career, Wright threw the full weight of his creative intelligence into the project. The massive brick and steel structure was designed to stand up to the heavy industrial architecture that surrounded it, yet the light-filled five-story atrium provided a pleasant interior environment for the 1,800 Larkin employees. Although more famous for its bold forms and progressive mechanical equipment, the central space was also inspiring. One worker recalled an "almost magical aura of calmness and order within the Larkin light court, despite the activity of so many office workers."

Although likely not the very first, as he claimed, Wright was probably one of the first architects in the country to introduce air conditioning, fireproofing, plate glass windows, open office planning, workstation furniture, and wall-hung toilets. His client wanted to promote an enthusiastic work ethic among the employees, and Wright adorned his atrium balconies with aphorisms exhorting initiative, loyalty, imagination, and generosity. But the employees were given more than lip service and indirect natural light. The office building had innovative spaces throughout for workers to spend their breaks and lunch hours: a library, classrooms, and a roof terrace. The social concerns of the owners were clearly expressed in the openness of the building's architectural forms.

As time goes on, Elwood continues to add more detail —furniture, plants, people—to his model. And as time brings greater computing power at lower prices, his medium of expression may change also. Now displayed in still images and on video, the Larkin Building model may eventually be put into a virtual reality format so that viewers can navigate and explore it at will. So, for modern visitors, this architectural treasure is not totally lost. We can recapture the sense of walking through a Wright original, even if we may never completely understand the reasons for its tragic demise.

Elwood modeled the Larkin Administration Building in AutoCAD, rendered it in 3D Studio, and performed additional image manipulations in Photoshop and Adobe Premiere.

A rooftop terrace provided a warm-weather lunching spot for employees. The amenities for workers were as revolutionary at the time as the building itself.

ASK AND IT SHALL BE GIVEN YOU
SEEK AND YE SHALL FIND KNOCK
AND IT SHALL BE OPENED UNTO YOU

The central light court was both
comfortable and inspiring for the
1,800 Larkin employees. Wright
adorned the atrium balconies with
aphorisms exhorting the virtues of
intelligence, enthusiasm, and control.

Frank Lloyd Wright's Larkin Administration Building was an early masterpiece of modernism, tragically destroyed in 1950. This recreation by Kenneth Elwood revives the character as well as the detail of the remarkable building.

From the main space, steps lead up to the annex library. Books and skylights made this a pleasant place for workers to enjoy their breaks.

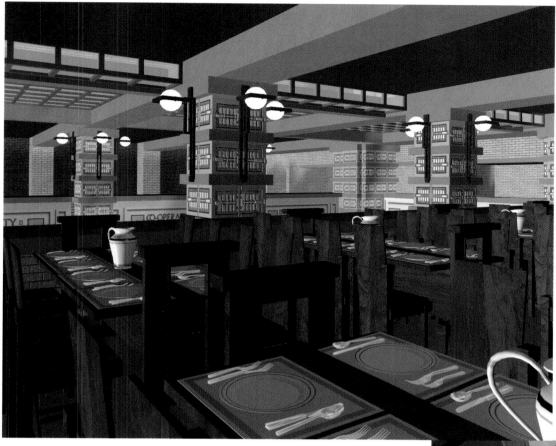

Views from the lunchroom and classrooms look out over the roof and into the central light court.

The interior of the Glashaus featured brightly colored tiles and an artificial waterfall.

To today's observer accustomed to space-age materials, a glass-domed pavilion might appear to be nothing out of the ordinary. But in 1914, when the German architect Bruno Taut built a glass house for the Werkbund Exhibition in Cologne, sculpting glass into such avant-garde forms was considered quite radical. The pavilion was a temporary structure, intended to demonstrate the flexibility of glass as a sculptural design element. Unfortunately, it was taken down within the year.

The Glashaus: An Experiment with Color and Glass

The Glashaus by Bruno Taut was a showcase for the use of glass. It was built for the 1914 Werkbund Exhibition in Cologne.

Taut was known for his dual love of functional simplicity and the play of color, and his work made an important break with nineteenth-century German architecture. The fourteen-sided Glashaus had walls of glass block and flat, diamond-shaped colored glass panels fitted into a concrete, dome-shaped space frame. Inside were an artificial waterfall and a metal staircase leading to the top of the dome. Brilliantly colored tiles and a mechanical kaleidoscope brightened the interior.

The photographs dating from 1914 reveal little of this color, but a new computer model demonstrates the play of color and light within the structure. It was modeled and rendered by Ilaria Mazzoleni, Jennifer Charleston, and Sarah Heyenbruch, students at the University of Southern California in Los Angeles under the direction of professor Karen Kensek. Mazzoleni notes that this small but significant building is a masterpiece of glass architecture. "Two of Taut's strongest ideas," she says, "were to use glass to liberate architecture from heavy elements and to integrate colors in the design. His powerful use of those ideas make him known in Europe as one of the most important avant-garde architects of the early twentieth century."

The dome of the Glashaus was a spectacle of light and color.

A pavilion designed by American architect Frank Lloyd Wright in cooperation with Canadian architect Francis Conroy Sullivan for the Banff National Park in Alberta, Canada, was surrounded by controversy during most of its short twenty-five-year life.

The Banff Park Pavilion:
Lost Gem of the Rockies

Tragically destroyed in 1938, when Wright was perhaps not as revered as he is today, the pavilion was said to be a prime example of his Prairie style. Located high in the Canadian Rocky Mountains, the single-story building was crafted of local fieldstone and rough-sawn woods. Its low-pitched roofs, deep overhangs, striking horizontality, leaded-glass windows, and orientation to the sun are all among Wright's signature features. One long, continuously glazed wall faced southwest to a terrace and the beautiful Borgeau Range beyond. The rustic interior, exposed roof truss, large fireplaces, covered balconies, and breathtaking view made it popular (eventually) with park visitors.

Controversy about the pavilion began when it was commissioned in 1911 by the Canadian Department of the Interior. Local residents wanted a simple, utilitarian sports arena. Government officials had something more refined in mind, and they got their way. Wright's design was simple yet elegant. The role of his associate Sullivan was probably to negotiate Canadian red tape, create the construction drawings, and supervise construction. But the design concept was pure Wright.

The building became the darling of well-to-do picnickers from the nearby city of Calgary. The citizens of Banff continued to resent the pavilion's presence as a symbol of the federal government's ignoring local needs. But its gradual undoing was more the fault of nature. On several occasions, the nearby Bow River flooded and weakened the structure. The exact circumstances of the building's destruction in 1938 are unknown. It may have been deliberately demolished because of the structural damage; it may have been accidentally destroyed due to misunderstandings by the repair crew. In any case, it was a loss to Canada and to architectural history. Sadly, it took years after its demolition before this was completely appreciated.

Now, for the first time in sixty years, the 14,000-square-foot (1300-square-meter) building has come alive again. University of Manitoba professor and architect Brian Sinclair, MRAIC, working with colleague Terence J. Walker, produced a computer model of the building to demonstrate the possibility of resurrecting lost treasures. They drew from original construction documents, hand sketches, photographs, physical models, and written descriptions from sources contemporary with the building. Unfortunately, this information does not constitute a complete picture. Because the building was small and remote from large population centers, it did not receive the attention other Wright buildings of that time may have enjoyed. And in 1913, when its construction began, common practice in architecture firms was to draw less and rely on craftsmen more. The construction drawings, therefore, are few and only lightly detailed. Furthermore, some of the historic material is contradictory, and Sinclair had to resolve discrepancies through historic research and architectural interpretation.

But drawing from a variety of sources, he and Walker were able to reproduce on the computer the principal architectural elements. For the exact appearance of materials Sinclair used photographs of local wood and stone, of materials from other Wright buildings, and illustrations from manufacturers' catalogs of the day. He then "mapped" these textures onto the model's surfaces to create a sense of realism. The result is a completely plausible reproduction, one that gives viewers a better sense of being there than any photograph or drawing could. "A limitation of traditional media," Sinclair says, "is its static or inert nature. Photographs, for example, reflect particular viewpoints determined by their creators— in effect placing a filter between the environment and our understanding of it." Through his computer model, and with the simulation of light and color, he hopes to evoke the feelings of those who were once able to walk around inside the building. Of course, we'll never again be able to enjoy the pavilion directly, but this brings us close.

Sinclair and Walker worked with AutoCAD and MiniCad to create 2D drawings, form·Z to model in three dimensions, and StudioPro for rendering. They have begun creating interactive walkthroughs to further enhance the experience of being inside the Banff Park Pavilion.

The southwest façade of the Banff Park Pavilion displays a strong horizontality. An expanse of leaded glass looks over the terrace to the mountains beyond.

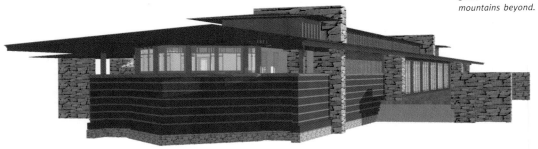

The northeast façade of Wright's pavilion featured a porte-cochere for arriving visitors. Its horizontality was punctuated by massive piers and fireplaces of local fieldstone.

The computer model with its roof removed reveals the patterns of heavy wood trusses and banks of leaded-glass windows and clerestories.

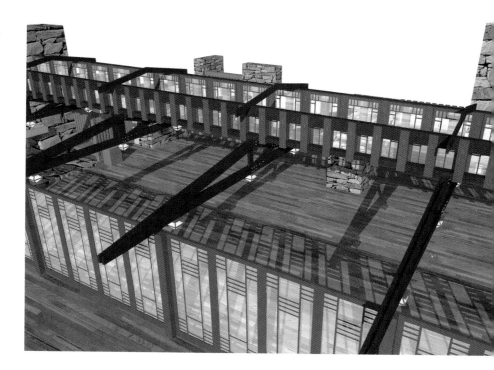

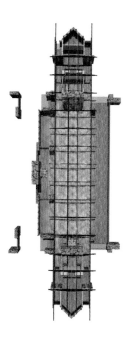

An aerial view of the model shows the Banff Park Pavilion in plan. The simple, elongated building had a porte-cochere and entrance to the northeast and a terrace to the southwest. In its day, it could accommodate three simultaneous picnics.

Part II:
Unbuilt Designs of Famous Architects

Throughout history, creative architects have been internally motivated to design even without a commission to produce a real building. Or perhaps they had a commission, but the client, for one reason or another, failed to have the project actually built. Or perhaps the architect wanted to make an ideological point and used the design for illustrative purposes only.

Many of these architects left drawings, in some cases quite detailed ones. More often, though, an unbuilt design is documented in only one or two sketches. In these cases, modern reconstructors have limited certainty that they are recreating the building as the master envisioned it. Viewers must be aware, especially when studying views not included in those one or two sketches, that what they are seeing is, to a great extent, created from the imagination of the reconstructor and from his or her knowledge of the architect's design style.

The examples in this section range from cathedrals of the sixteenth-century Italian architect Baldassarre Peruzzi to a mile-high skyscraper by Frank Lloyd Wright. Also included are early-twentieth-century architects Antonio Sant'Elia, Le Corbusier, and Iakov Chernikov. These buildings all give students of architectural history fresh material in understanding the creative minds of the masters. In a unique academic study of the Renaissance master Andrea Palladio, we see two Italian villas that Palladio didn't actually design, but might have.

Frank Lloyd Wright was commissioned in 1958 to design the Trinity Chapel for the University of Oklahoma. The triangular structure, never built, was to have been of poured concrete and stained glass. These images were produced by Jennifer Charleston, an architecture student at the University of Southern California.

Peter Parsons, reconstructor of the Peruzzi work, has been compared to Paul Letarouilly. This nineteenth-century Frenchman published perspective sketches of Rome that captured the character of spaces, in contrast to the then-prevailing custom of illustrating buildings only in plan and elevation. Letarouilly's drawings were popular among Europeans who couldn't travel but were intrigued by Rome's architectural wonders. Similarly, Parsons and the others in this section enlivened the designs they've reconstructed and now help us travel to a past that never happened.

Italian architect Baldassarre Peruzzi was so highly regarded in the sixteenth century that when he died he was buried in the Parthenon beside the famous artist Raphael. But although Peruzzi mastered many of the arts and sciences, he neglected the art of self-promotion and is relatively unknown today.

Reviving Peruzzi: An Old Master Returns to Fame

Now that is changing, thanks to the computer modeling work of Peter Parsons, an architecture professor at Rensselaer Polytechnic Institute in Troy, New York. Parsons brought to life several designs that Peruzzi developed around 1531 for the reconstruction of the church of San Domenico in Siena, which had been partially destroyed by fire. Sadly for Siena and for architectural history, none of Peruzzi's designs for this church were ever built, probably for financial reasons. But the surviving drawings, stored in the Uffizi Gallery in Florence, provided Parsons with the information needed to model the proposed reconstructions.

Parsons's renderings of the church's interior give a sense of what the building would have been like had it been built.

Parsons began by scanning copies of Peruzzi's original sketches into the computer. With special software, he traced over the scanned plans and elevations, creating 2D templates. These templates became the base drawings for the 3D models, from which he rendered many interior views.

The resulting images change the perspective offered by Peruzzi's flat drawings. "These images capture the experience of being there," Parsons says. When seen in the context of medieval Siena, they also demonstrate Peruzzi's mastery of urban planning. Parsons explains, "The vaulted domes and combinations of archways and columns would have given the church some grandeur and would have tied it visually and architecturally to the great cathedral that stands on the opposing hill."

In another project that is helping to rehabilitate Peruzzi's reputation, Parsons used his scholarship to solve a mystery

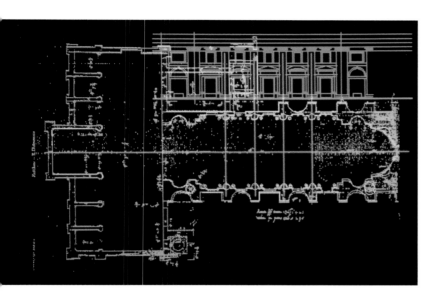

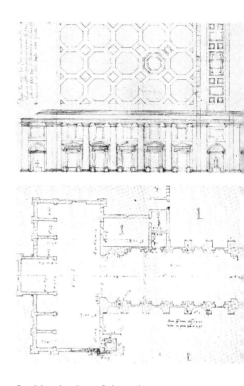

Surviving drawings of sixteenth-century Italian architect Baldassarre Peruzzi provided architect Peter Parsons with the data he needed to reconstruct the Church of San Domenico, originally designed to be built in Siena.

of architectural history. Traditionally, historians have believed that a set of drawings that combined studies of ancient Roman ruins with designs for a church somehow related to Peruzzi's designs for Saint Peter's in Rome and dated to the late years of his life. Parsons, however, demonstrated that the drawings were early works and indeed preliminary studies for the 1514 design for the cathedral at Carpi. At first glance they seem unrelated to the cathedral. When viewed in light of the linear design methodologies of modern architects, they seem to be for different projects altogether. But by overlaying computer images of the various drawings, Parsons demonstrated certain common characteristics. Their similarities illustrate Peruzzi's nonlinear, imaginative, and unique design method. Parsons concludes, "If Peruzzi had followed design process as it is traditionally taught, he would not have been able to create what he created." Parsons hopes that his research will instruct modern architects about Peruzzi and elevate this Renaissance master to the position in history he deserves.

When Parsons began this work a few years ago, he used CAD Overlay ESP for scanning and tracing the original plans and elevations, AutoCAD for creating templates, MegaMODEL for modeling, and MegaPAINT for rendering. More recently he modeled in form·Z and explored newer rendering possibilities.

In the sixteenth century, the famous Italian architect Andrea Palladio built a series of villas in the countryside near Venice. A student of ancient Roman architecture and fascinated with ideas of symmetry and proportion, Palladio developed a vocabulary of rules and patterns for these country estates. He didn't adhere rigidly to the rules; rather, he used them as a foundation from which to explore expression of form. Armed with his writings about these design principles and the body of his surviving work, architects in the twentieth century have been trying to understand the relationship between limiting rules and limitless expression.

A Possible Palladian Villa:
Understanding History through Technology

Recently they have begun using computer technology to aid their explorations. While human creativity can probably never be defined completely within a computer program, the process of trying to capture Palladio's design rules has refined our understanding of exactly what those rules are.

A Palladian house typically sported a formal portico and was flanked by barchesse that housed farm animals, workers, and grain. In front were a courtyard and garden.

The term *villa* in Palladio's day denoted more than a building; it meant the entire estate, including a house, outbuildings, and grounds. The house was a symmetrical one- or two-story structure with characteristically Roman features. A typical floor plan, with overall width-to-length proportions of between 1:1 and 1:2, consisted of a large, central, public room leading to a sequence of increasingly smaller and more private rooms on each side. The attic and basement, if any, were reserved for servants' quarters, workrooms, and storage. The houses themselves were relatively small but appeared larger because they were typically flanked by barchesse, or barnlike structures, that extended like wings beyond each side of the main house. These housed farm animals, workers, grain, and so on. In front of the house was a courtyard, and behind were formal gardens, orchards, and woods. Occupants of the villas were the landed gentry of Venice; they enjoyed a luxurious country life while their farms fed the city.

The attempt to categorize the patterns and principles that make up the villa designs began with Palladio himself. In his renowned *Four Books of Architecture* he outlined the principles he applied in creating his diverse but consistent villas. Rudolf Wittkower demonstrated in 1949 that the villas follow the pattern of a tartan grid—that is, the layout of rooms in plan

lies on a grid of horizontal and vertical lines that are unequally but symmetrically spaced. In the 1970s, William Mitchell and George Stiny applied this principle to define what seemed to be the complete set of schemes for villa plans that could be generated by Palladian grids. However, some of their schemes can be seen by the trained eye to be un-Palladian. In the 1980s, Yale researchers Richard Freedman and George Hersey developed a computer program that generated graphic plans and elevations. These drawings were based on Palladian principles and on the known frequency of certain design characteristics in Palladio's built legacy and the unbuilt work he described in *Four Books*. Their program also specifies window placement and column spacing for the porticos. They discovered additional rules that eliminate plans acceptable by Stiny and Mitchell's rules. For example, no room is as long or as wide as the plan; the total number of rooms is less than or equal to twenty; and the ratio of the smallest room to the largest is 1:9.

In the 1990s, Thomas Seebohm and his students at the University of Waterloo built on the Freedman-Hersey designs, translating the plans and elevations into 3D computer models. In selecting a few that looked the most Palladian, they discovered still more rules. For example, Seebohm noted, two or more identical rooms in a row are not allowed; the large central room must be on the perimeter or removed from the perimeter by at most a recessed portico; and the short side of a larger room is the long side of an adjacent smaller room. By applying the increasingly detailed rules and critiquing the un-Palladian characteristics at each step, Seebohm and his students developed several villas that Palladio himself might have designed. Seebohm says, "It is only possible to fully understand an architect's design principles when, after incorporating what one perceives to be these principles in a design, a building results which visually looks like a work of the architect being studied. The outcome of this

study is a *possible* Palladian villa, but the objective is not the villa but what can be learned along the way about Palladio's design intentions for villas."

He and his students went beyond looking only at the main house, as earlier researchers did, and developed the *barchesse*, courtyard, and gardens. This is very important to understanding the built environment of the villa because, as Palladio wrote 400 years ago, "pleasure gardens and kitchen gardens are the sole and the chief recreation of the villa." The resulting renderings succeed in making viewers feel they are in the middle of a Renaissance garden. Interestingly, Seebohm points

out that the formal gardens in Palladio's time, with their geometric sections, fountains, and manicured topiary, were laid out in grids similar to those of the main house.

In reviewing the models and the incremental process of discovery, Seebohm concludes, "Instead of being a passive observer, the student of architectural history is now able to experience, like our ancestors, which of all the possibilities open to us are relevant for our consideration and action. We've been able to display a reality recreated from the past into which we can project ourselves."

The Palladian villas were modeled in GDS and rendered in Radiance.

In a second Palladian model, the barchesse curves around to the front and the main house sports a domed roof.

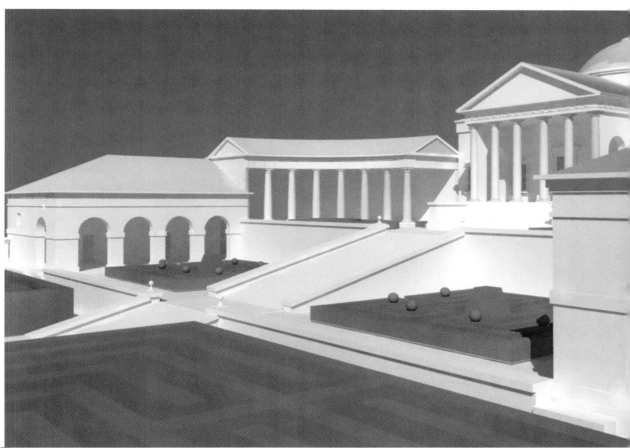

Palladian villas, such as this hypothetical one modeled by Thomas Seebohm and his students at the University of Waterloo, were more than a single building. The entire estate consisted of house, outbuildings, and formal gardens.

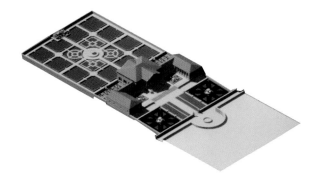

Early in the twentieth century, a young Italian architect began making a name for himself. By 1914, Antonio Sant'Elia was famous for his architectural vision of the future. Although little of his work was ever built, his drawings and writings remain influential. His publication, "Manifesto of Futurist Architecture", featured drawings of what he thought cities of the late century would look like.

The Legacy of Sant'Elia:
Back to the Future

One striking structure illustrated in the manifesto was his station for airplanes and trains. Considering that flight technology was still very young in his day, he was indeed visionary. It is sobering to contemplate his images and see how much of their monumental scale has become reality around the world.

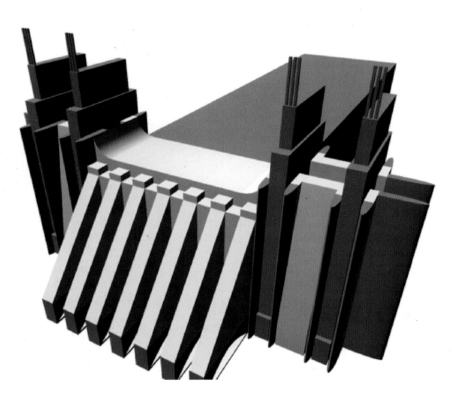

A 3D massing model was the second stage of the modeling process. Each component was gradually replaced with one of increasingly finer detail.

Midhat Delic, an architecture student at the University of Oregon, developed a fascination with Sant'Elia's vision and modeled the massive structure of the station for airplanes and trains. Delic modeled and rendered the station with form·Z. He based his model on the several sketches that Sant'Elia produced of the structure's exterior. To determine the scale, Delic used the few available clues, such as the size of the trains. He began by drawing diagrams of the spatial organization and hierarchy of structural forms. From these he created simple massing models and gradually added detail. He periodically compared 3D projections of his model to the views of the Sant'Elia drawings to make sure his reproduction was as close as possible to the architect's original idea. Knowing that a completely precise reproduction is impossible from fragmentary source material, Delic sought mainly to convey the feeling of the place. He chose to use primarily shades of gray, with only muted colors as highlights, despite the sophisticated rendering software at his disposal. "I kept the colors somber," he notes, "to indicate the gloom of this environment. Sant'Elia himself used little color." Unfortunately, there are no original sketches of the structure's interior or back elevation, so Delic left that up to our imagination.

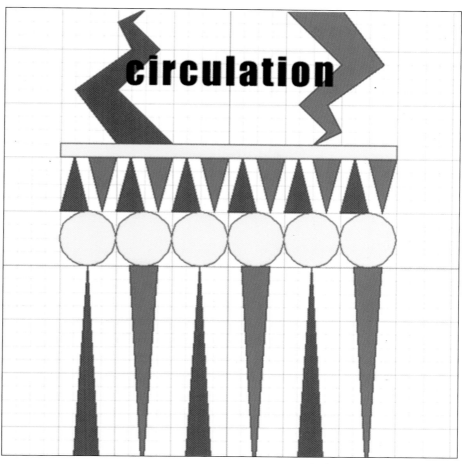

A simple 2D diagram of the circulation system was the first step for Midhat Delic in modeling Antonio Sant'Elia's station for airplanes and trains.

The station was conceived as a massive urban structure for the convergence of several forms of transportation. Train lines are at the lowest level, roads for automobiles are at the street level, and an airstrip is on the roof. Pedestrian walks are on overpasses, and funiculars and elevators transport people between levels. All this was imagined in a time when horse-drawn vehicles were more common than automobiles. Just a few years after his manifesto was published, Sant'Elia died a young hero in World War I. The term *futurism* unfortunately came to be tainted by its later association with fascism. But there is no doubt that the architect and his vision of a technological future were ahead of their time.

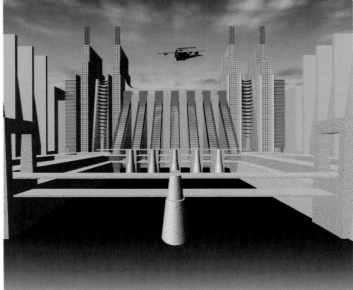

The imaginary station for airplanes and trains was the work of early-twentieth-century Italian futurist Antonio Sant'Elia. The massive structure featured train lines below grade, a landing strip at the top, and roadways and walkways in between.

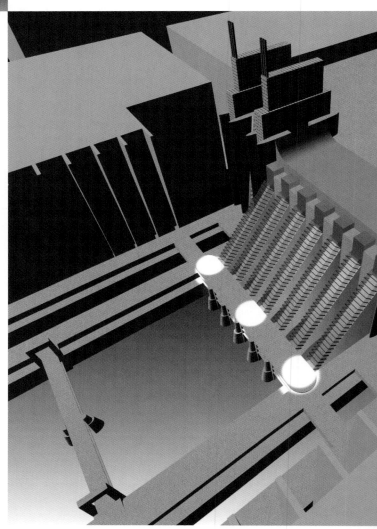

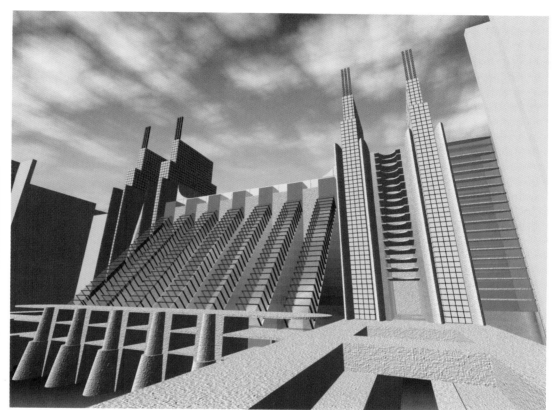

If Le Corbusier had lived in the late twentieth century, he might have dabbled in computer graphics in pursuit of geometric analysis and design. Instead, the famous French architect applied his influence during the middle of the century, and modern researchers are only now using computers to analyze his designs. Between 1922 and 1929, Le Corbusier developed a series of theoretical villas for the working classes.

Geometry to Live In: The Unrealized Villas of Le Corbusier

These were deceptively simple white cubist houses, often perched on thin columns to provide a work area below the main living space. During this purist period, he also published *Towards a New Architecture*, in which he outlined his vision for the built environment of the new century. His book refers to the geometric logic that underlies the villas' plans and elevations. None of the seven villas illustrated was ever built, but through computer models we are able to see what they might have been like.

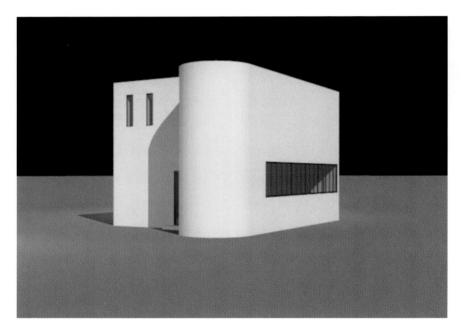

Maison d'Ouvrier

One key concept in Le Corbusier's design vocabulary is that of regulating lines. These are geometric abstractions that, when traced over a building's plan or elevation, demonstrate the proportional relationships of various architectural elements. These proportions, he argued, are what make architecture beautiful, and he used them to guide his purist compositions. In two dimensions, these regulating lines were squares and circles; in three dimensions, they were cubes, cylinders, and so on. They could be manipulated through rotating, mirroring, and resizing to create an infinite number of related design variations.

One interesting proportion Le Corbusier used frequently is the so-called *golden rectangle*. This harmonious shape can endlessly repeat itself. Designers have long used such generative shapes and forms to create new buildings and researchers have used them to analyze existing ones. Jerzy Wojtowicz, an architecture professor at the University of British Columbia in Canada, applied these forms with computer drawing and modeling software to understand and reconstruct Le Corbusier's unbuilt villas. Many of the villas were originally documented with only one or two sketches. In the process of modeling, Wojtowicz occasionally

Le Corbusier's Maison d'Artiste shown from twelve views simulates the impression one gets from walking around the VRML model of the villa.

   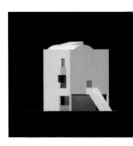

A geometric proportion Le Corbusier used frequently is the so-called golden rectangle. Bisect a square into two equal rectangles. Draw the diagonal of one of those rectangles and, with that diagonal as a radius, extend an arc down to the rectangle's base. Extend the base line until it intersects the arc to get the long side of the golden rectangle. The side of the original square is the short side of the rectangle. This proportion is not only intrinsically harmonious in its appearance, it is also generative of other rectangles in the same proportion. Take the long side of the golden rectangle and use that measure to draw a new, larger square. That square combined with the first golden rectangle is another golden rectangle. Similarly, subtract a square from any golden rectangle to create another, smaller golden rectangle. The harmonious shape can endlessly repeat itself.

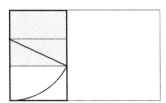

relied on regulating lines to make educated guesses about what Le Corbusier had intended. That selected renderings of his models look like the original sketches reinforces the idea of how important the regulating lines were in developing the original designs. The models in turn display the underlying geometric logic as well as the experience of walking around unbuilt masterpieces.

In spite of the geometric simplicity and logic of these villas, Wojtowicz insists they are not formulaic. Le Corbusier did not apply design rules mechanistically but used them in service to his personal expression. Yet the computational methods Wojtowicz used were instrumental to his ability to model the villas. He concludes, "Information technology affords us the opportunity to construct complex interactive models, thus enhancing our understanding of the designed object."

Wojtowicz modeled these villas with AutoCAD and Wavefront Advanced Visualizer running on a Silicon Graphics workstation.

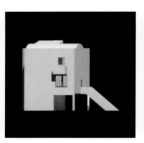

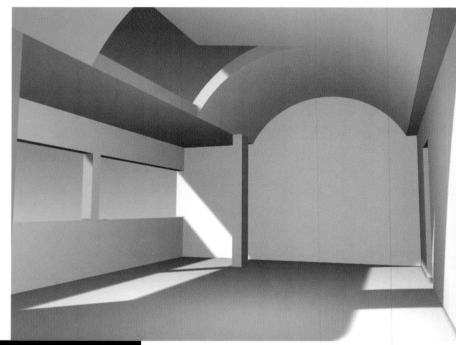

Maison d'Artiste

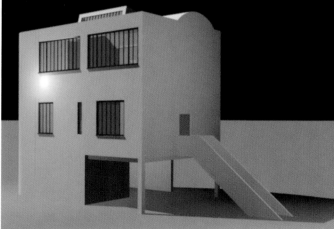

An interior view of the Maison d'Artiste showing the circular regulating lines that shape the curved ceiling.

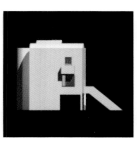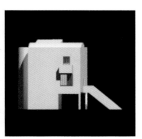

Maison et Cantine

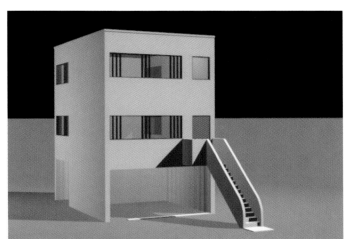

Maison et Cantine

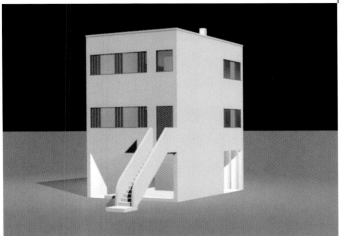

Maison Baizeau

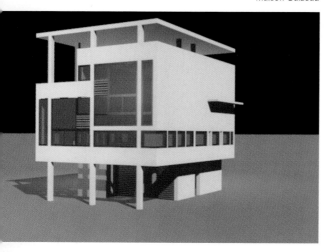

Villa Ribot

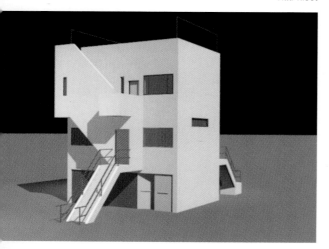

Maison Jacquin

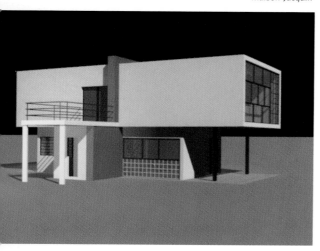

Jerzy Wojtowicz modeled seven unbuilt villas designed by the famous French architect Le Corbusier in the 1920s. Four elevations for each villa are shown here. From top to bottom: Maison d'Ouvrier, Maison d'Artiste, Villa Ribot, Maison et Cantine, Maison Canale, Maison Jacquin, and Maison Baizeau.

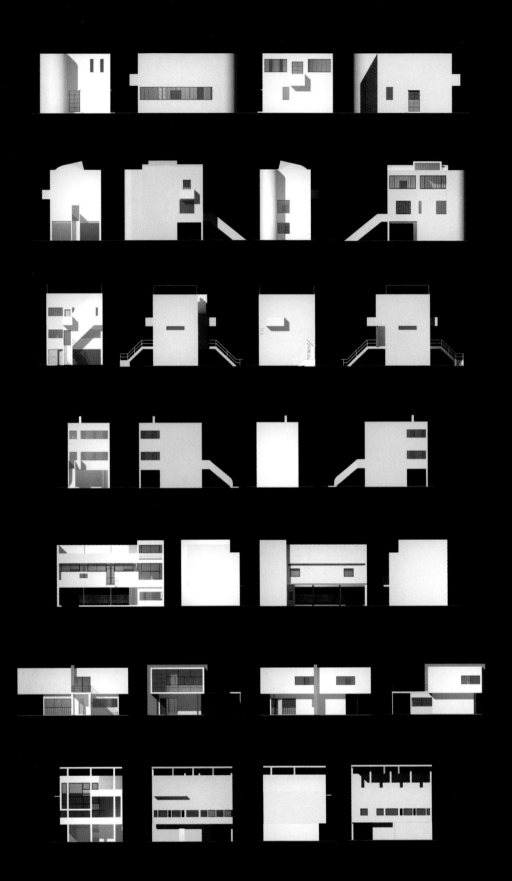

When Iakov Chernikhov drafted his visions of early-twentieth-century Russian industrial architecture, was he drawing buildable structures or exercising artistic license to create a dramatic effect? Because it is uncertain if any of Chernikhov's published designs were ever built, we may never know the answer to these questions. But for several years they have been studied by professor of architecture Thomas Seebohm and his students at the University of Waterloo in Ontario, Canada. By translating the Russian's drawings into 3D computer models, Seebohm has been able to further demonstrate Chernikhov's design vision and speculate about how realistic they are geometrically.

Chernikhov's Constructivism: Fact or Fiction?

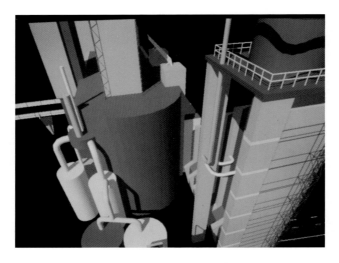

Constructivist architects, known for their work immediately after the Russian revolution, were interested in buildings that were functional, rational, and purposeful, buildings that expressed their construction and reflected a progressive new era rooted in industry and technology. Chernikhov, while incorporating constructivist tendencies, was never really a part of the movement. For him, constructivism was the expression of beauty as an artistic idea conveyed through a language of forms and their spatial relationships. In other words, the feeling symbolized by a building was created by his choice of forms and how they fit together. His vocabulary of forms and spatial relationships as applied to various building types is illustrated in his book,

Iakov Chernikhov published his visions of early-twentieth-century Russian industrial architecture as 101 Architectural Fantasies *in 1933. The first image in each set of three was rendered to match the view in Chernikhov's book. Fantasy 4 was modeled by Ivo Valentik.*

101 *Architectural Fantasies*, published in 1933. Because all of Chernikhov's books were intended to teach formal design principles to a new generation of architects, it is possible that his fantasies fall more in the realm of graphic art than that of constructible architecture. His images portray a brave new world of industrial imagery that may have been meant more to inspire that new generation than to instruct them in practical construction. Some of them are bird's-eye views of complex, abstract cityscapes that resemble science fiction scenes to the modern eye. Others, including those Seebohm chose to study, are viewed from the ground, thus exaggerating the relative height of the towering vertical elements. These images include single buildings or clusters of buildings, with huge cross-braced steel trusses and massive concrete frames.

Because Chernikhov drew each fantasy from only one viewpoint, it is geometrically impossible to interpret them with certainty. Seebohm used the laws of perspective to show that one view could be interpreted to represent many possible geometric configurations. To go beyond this impasse, he worked on the assumption that Chernikov chose a viewpoint in each case that would align with the most prominent vertical features and therefore maximize the dramatic exaggeration of the building's central focus of interest. By drawing on other cues in the drawings, Seebohm made inferences about the portions of the building not seen in the originals. He and his students thus discovered occasional anomalies in the designs. Two towers, for example, that on first glance appeared to be twins, could be demonstrated to be of different sizes. If Chernikhov had drawn an accurate perspective of twin towers, the image would not have had nearly as dramatic an effect. This revelation strengthened Seebohm's suspicion that Chernikhov's goal was effect, not geometric accuracy.

Each student modeler was asked to develop one rendered view corresponding to an original drawing. To further study the design, the students then projected additional views of the models. They discovered that, in many cases, the original view was the most advantageous in dramatizing the building, further reinforcing the notion that Chernikhov was more interested in effect than fact. Seebohm notes, "It's possible that some of these conclusions could have been reached without the use of 3D computer modeling. But with only a sound understanding of the theory of perspective drawing, our experience indicates that modeling helped to bring the conclusions into focus more directly than would otherwise have been the case. These models allowed us to see the effects of moving architectural components, and hence to demonstrate Chernikhov's distortions for the sake of the drawing." In addition, the models allowed the researchers to see Chernikhov's architecture from a variety of viewpoints and to conclude that the architecture was designed for the sake of the drawings, not vice versa. And, Seebohm concludes, "this study shows how misleading a few isolated views of a building can be."

Whether or not the less dramatic views of Chernikhov's designs add much to our knowledge of architectural history, one thing is fairly certain. Now that computer modeling is available to probe the forms implied in historic drawings, history will be able to hold architects more accountable for the perspectives they construct or to illuminate why they distorted them.

The students modeled the Chernikhov fantasies in AutoCAD or form·Z and Seebohm rendered them with GDS software.

Chernikhov's Fantasy 39, by Ajay Mistry, Wayne Lee, Bob Abrahams, and James Wu. The second view is a hypothetical side wing not visible in Chernikhov's drawing.

Chernikhov's Fantasy 42, by Jeff Zavitz, Sandy Chan, and James Wu.

Chernikhov's Fantasy 93, by Louis-Charles Lasnier, Mark Sider, Filip Simpson, and Ari Wahl. The third view is a hypothetical side wing not visible in Chernikhov's drawing.

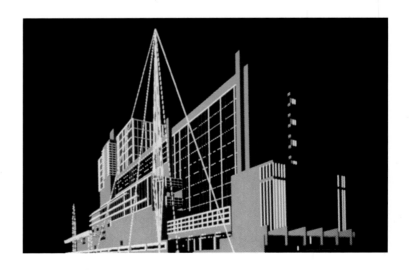

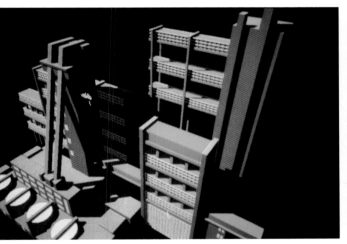

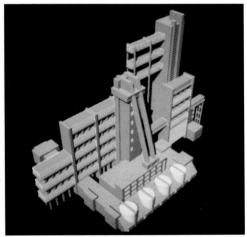

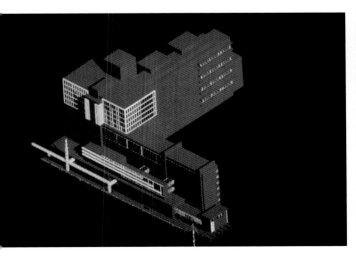

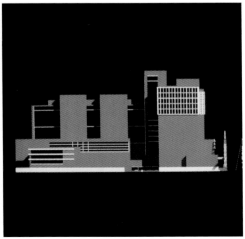

We will probably never know if Frank Lloyd Wright seriously believed he could build a skyscraper a mile in height. But his drawings and writings make him sound convinced of the project's constructibility. Dubbed "The Illinois," this structure was unveiled in sketches at a testimonial dinner in Wright's honor in 1956, just a few years before his death.

The Illinois Building:
Wright's Mile-High Fantasy

The 528-story building embodies many then-modern materials and construction processes. It is tripod-shaped for stability, embedded deep into bedrock, built of steel, and sheathed in metal and glass. In a gesture that seems ironic to the modern environmentalist, each face of the building was detailed differently to take best advantage of the solar energy that arrived from different angles. Yet Wright relied on "atomic energy" to power the necessarily extensive elevator system.

The Illinois was part of Usonia, Wright's vision for an idealized and harmonious convergence of city and landscape. The skyscraper, which Wright predicted could support a population of 130,000, sat in the middle of a landscape of freeways, multi-story parking garages, and self-steering, flying-saucerlike "taxi-copters" that Wright expected would run on radio beams. Unlike modern visions of architecture in harmony with nature, this building would have been high-tech and high-energy. And highly unlikely to work. The technical challenges of building a structure so tall are probably insurmountable. Today, on the eve of the millennium, forty years after Wright's death, the tallest building in the world is only a fraction of this height.

Frank Lloyd Wright's 1956 vision of Usonia included a mile-high skyscraper and radio-powered "taxi-copters" set harmoniously in the American landscape.

Nevertheless, the vision of Usonia captures the imagination and is surely part of the reason we remember Frank Lloyd Wright as one of the most visionary architects of the twentieth century. Among his admirers are four graduate students at Columbia

At the base of the skyscraper sits the landing pad for the taxi-copters, of Wright's invention.

University's Graduate School of Architecture, Planning, and Preservation who have modeled, rendered, and animated the skyscraper and its surroundings. Urs Britschgi, Mike Hsu, Ashley Schafer, and Max Strang worked together in the school's Digital Design Lab on this mammoth independent study project. Their modeling includes several other unbuilt Wright projects, such as the Rogers Lacy Hotel, the Pittsburgh Civic Center, and the Point Park Bridge. They write, "Wright's vision for the American landscape was an alternative to America's urban ills. He proposed a balanced synthesis of architecture and landscape that would stretch from coast to coast."

Just as we'll probably never test The Illinois's constructibility, we'll never know if this synthesis was actually harmonious or if it can cure urban ills. But projects like this can help us fantasize about futures that will never be.

The students worked with Silicon Graphics workstations and SoftImage software, and premiered at the SIGGRAPH '97 Computer Animation Festival in Los Angeles.

The Illinois had at its base a complex of freeways, bridges, and multistory parking garages.

The Illinois was tripod in shape to give it the strength needed to support its one-mile in height.

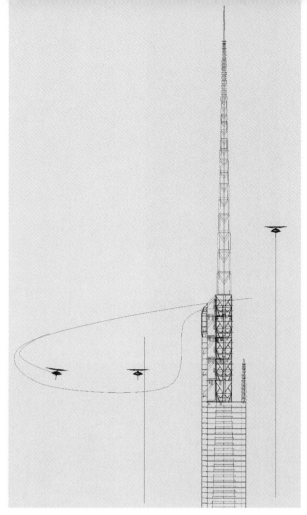

An elevation drawing of The Illinois
shows the building's trusslike structure
and the flight paths of the taxi-copters.

Taxi-copters transported passengers
to higher-level "sky lobbies" as a
faster alternative to the atomic-
powered elevator system.

An interior atrium in The Illinois.

Part III:
Designing from the Imagination

There are many reasons besides human habitation for designing and modeling buildings. Some architects develop digital environments for computer games. Some build models simply as a vehicle for learning how to use the modeling software. Most likely, though, today's largest source of 3D architectural models created explicitly for buildings that will never be built is the architecture school design studio. The studio is traditionally at the core of the professional curriculum. It is a course taken repeatedly throughout a student's architectural education, aimed at integrating the skills of drawing, analysis, and design. Typically, students are given architectural programs—not to be confused with computer programs—that specify the required functional, social, technical, and civic elements of a building. They then spend several weeks or months developing a proposed building to respond to these needs. Professors assign problems like office buildings and fire stations to expose students to design challenges that they are likely to face professionally. Increasingly, over the last decade, studios have integrated computer modeling with traditional drawing and design processes, so modeling becomes an important new skill set in the students' repertoire. Some of the most imaginative designs are inspired not by ordinary programs but by design competitions and imaginary places students read about in books.

In the hands of students experienced in the wide range of available software, the design process becomes a fertile manipulation of media. Like a master painter with a limitless palette of colors, these students learn not only how to use various media but also how to decide when a particular medium is appropriate. They may use simple 2D drawing software to make preliminary sketches, for example, then move to 3D modeling later in the process when the building becomes developed enough to require study in three dimensions. They may go directly from hand sketches to 3D modeling and rely on the modeling software to generate plans, elevations, and sections. Or they may create concepts working directly in the 3D modeling environment.

Whatever the sequence, a designer thoroughly comfortable with the available media will not feel limited to digital tools. Instead, he or she may move back and forth between hand sketching and computer drawing without sensing any discontinuity of design thinking. It is common, for example, for designers early in their development of a project to construct a simple massing model on the computer, portraying only the major volumes. They then print out a perspective image and use pencil or watercolor to add detail. The result combines the precision of the computer-generated perspective with the loose,

Brian Dell, Faiza Malik, and Terence Yan, students of Darlene Brady at the University of Illinois at Urbana/ Champaign, created this model of the fictitious seaside city of Despina from Italo Calvino's novel Invisible Cities.

liberating discovery-through-sketching that is generally considered easiest with manual media.

As budding architects design buildings for practice, many explore radically new design processes made possible by computer technology. These young people have a tremendous potential influence over the future of the profession. A new generation of students

has never known life without computers, and their ease with the tool gives them an advantage over seasoned professionals in exploiting the technology.

Architecture students who use computers in their design studios learn that the tool has more to offer than efficiency through automation. When they build 3D models of their projects, they receive more and better visual feedback than from manual methods. Networked with other students, their capacity to collaborate increases. In general, their greater access to information and input yields more thoughtful, more highly developed designs.

An International Airport:
Opportunities for Collaboration

At the University of Waterloo, the students of John Shnier, Philip Beesley, and Thomas Seebohm demonstrated these benefits in the design of a new international airport for the Greater Toronto Airport Authority. The project was intended to parallel the real design underway for the Lester B. Pearson Airport, which is expected to accommodate an increase from twenty million passengers annually to fifty million by the year 2020. The students were asked to consider the many complex technical and cultural design issues inherent in any airport—circulation, security, the movement of massive numbers of passengers and suitcases—without sacrificing architectural quality and civic identity. In addition, Shnier, Beesley, and Seebohm challenged the students to imbue their design with a thematic character strong enough to predominate over the mix of many small elements. Is the airport an inward-looking symbol of the city or an outward-looking gateway to the rest of the world? How does one design a place that is both machinelike in efficiency yet able to soothe the emotional highs and lows that travelers may experience?

The students worked in teams of three to develop schemes that would satisfy the complex set of sometimes contradictory needs. One team—Andrew Mannion, Christopher Ono, and Kevin Stelzer—chose to work with a linear scheme whereby they separated the terminal from departure and arrival gates in both space and time. Their terminal is a large public area, accessible to all, where surface transportation arrives, passengers check their bags, and families reunite in a noisy bustle of activity. Then, after passing through security and customs, departing passengers take leave of the tension-filled terminal and board a train to an island on the tarmac where they await their flights. This quiet, light-filled space offers opportunities for observation and contemplation.

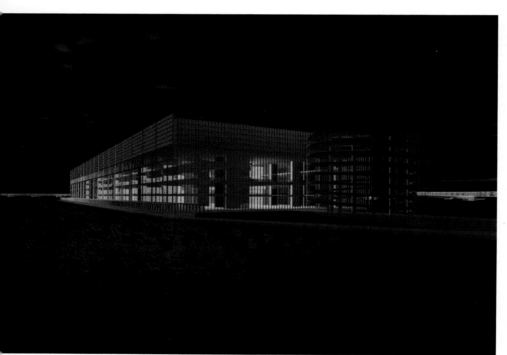

The terminal building of an international airport designed by University of Waterloo students Andrew Mannion, Christopher Ono, and Kevin Stelzer is a large, bustling, high-ceilinged public area.

Interestingly, this separation of functions in the airport also supported a division of labor among the three design students. While one worked on the terminal, another worked on the satellite; a third worked out details of an escalator. Because the computer model was, in effect, a digital database of information about the building rather than just a collection of drawings, it could be shared and managed more effectively, thus accelerating the design process. After a time, the work could rotate, with each of the three further developing the design of his classmate. This increased opportunity for redesign subjected the model to a greater range of creative ideas and instilled confidence in the designers as they progressed.

This sharing ultimately improved the quality of the overall design, according to Stelzer. "It might sound trite to talk about the efficiency benefits of the computer in design," he says. "But if you structure a model so that small changes can be repeated throughout the building auto-matically and visibly, you can spend your time and attention on other issues. From the beginning we used virtual models to test spatial concepts. In this project, ambient light was an important issue. In addition to merely simulating the desired conditions of space and light, we are starting to integrate the computer as a medium to evoke associations and emotion."

Another student team of airport designers took a different approach. They began with the hypothesis that an airport is a nonplace. By this they meant that, unlike other public spaces, airports are not identified by their history or cultural or commercial activity—rather, they are areas of transience where passengers focus on what was left behind and what is to come. This team called their scheme "paring away the inessentials," meaning that the design focused on the primary functions of air transportation, where architectural features made the building's functions explicit. This reduced the need for signage while making it easier for travelers to find their way. The overall design of the airport was a matrix embodying circulation systems such as internal roads, the train leading to satellites, and moving sidewalks. The ability to create accurate perspectives that showed the true play of light in, and transparency through, the spaces enabled the students to test their design for the architectural clarity demanded by their hypothesis.

The airport designs shown here include the linear scheme of the Mannion/Ono/Stelzer team and a radial scheme of the team of Monty King, Janet Lee, and Kendall Wayow.

Natasha Lebel, Rene Sellier, and Trevor McIvor designed the paring-away-the-inessentials scheme. The students modeled their airports in form·Z, rendered them in Radiance, and further developed plans and other ortho-graphic drawings in AutoCAD. Although computing played an important role in the development of all the projects, the students tried to find the appropriate balance of hand and computer techniques. Two of the final presentations included both computer models and physical models.

*By contrast, the satellite buildings
for the arrival and departure gates
provide quiet, light-filled spaces
and opportunities for observation
and contemplation.*

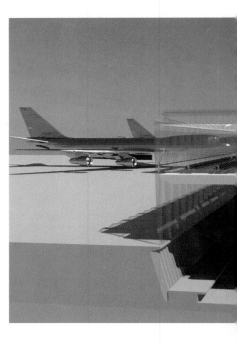

The paring-away-the-inessentials scheme for the airport, designed by Natasha Lebel, Rene Sellier, and Trevor McIvor, focused on the primary functions of commercial air transportation, where architectural features made the building's functions explicit.

A third scheme, radial in nature, was designed by University of Waterloo students Monty King, Janet Lee, and Kendall Wayow.

Even when the design goal of a student project is as ordinary as an office building, the means for achieving design excellence can be greatly enriched through digital imagery. At the University of Oregon, Professor Daniel Herbert and his students explore image manipulation as a technique for expanding the capabilities of traditional drawing techniques.

Serendipity in Design:
New Methods from New Technologies

Francis Dardis, now a practicing architect in Portland, conducted several such experiments while a master's student at Oregon. In two advanced studio projects he developed techniques for moving imagery back and forth between traditional drawings and models and computer representations. He found that the resulting imagery was far richer and more evocative than conventional media normally were.

Dardis's first project was a medium-rise office building. With the Spanish architect Gaudi as his inspiration, Dardis sought a façade without repetition but based on a regular structural system. He built a small conceptual model out of Mylar and balsa wood, then placed this directly on a computer scanner. He then took the scanned image into Adobe Photoshop, where he subjected it to a variety of filters that performed such manipulations as adjusting contrast, adding textures, blurring lines, changing colors, and so on. Unlike the manipulations that students typically do by hand with pencil and tracing paper, these often resulted in images that were totally unexpected. More often than not, the unexpected images were uninteresting, but a few turned out to be visually attractive and intellectually stimulating. When Dardis tried to understand the images in light of the real-world issues of functional program, social context, and construction technology that every architectural designer must confront, he felt that the abstractions were informing his design. This rich imagery was giving him ideas for developing the design's form and structure in directions he was unlikely to have found in his own imagination.

Dardis and Herbert analyzed the cognitive processes students go through when they conduct such schematic design explorations. They came up with several explanations for the techniques' effectiveness in expanding the design horizons of student designers. For one, the digital imagery tends to resemble physical surfaces, in contrast to lines and edges that more commonly characterize student sketches. The color and textures of these surfaces are more complex and evocative of architecture than black-and-white

In an experimental design process for an office building, then-student Francis Dardis applied an unusual combination of computer techniques. He began by building a small conceptual model from Mylar and balsa wood and placing it directly on a computer scanner.

He then manipulated the scanned image with various filters in Adobe Photoshop and selected the few results that he found interesting.

lines. Students are able to read more into them and to find meaning amid the chaos and ambiguity of the abstractions. This complexity grows throughout a series of manipulations, whereas traditional media imagery becomes more precise over time. And because the images are unexpected, designers may find themselves startled by new ideas they would never have found within their usual repertoire. The ambiguity in the abstractions forces designers to stretch their imaginations in the effort to bring sense to the chaos. Of course, the tireless ability of the computer to generate many variations very quickly means that designers have a wealth of images to choose from.

In a second project, Dardis undertook the design of a forest-research complex, including many buildings and the surrounding campus. He began with charcoal sketches of vague ideas he had about wooden structures resembling trees reaching up as fingers to support a roof. Setting those sketches aside, he next built a site model, scanned it, and applied a series of filters. To his amazement, one result (a site plan) bore an uncanny resemblance to one of the

early charcoal sketches (a building section). Whether it was coincidence or an unconscious development, the convergence of these two images clicked for him and he knew he was on track. Professor Herbert refers to such phenomena as "nonlinear shifts in the design process." They contrast sharply with the deliberate, conscious explorations that designers usually carry out with manual media.

Importantly, the texture of the images, which would have been difficult or impossible to draw by hand, helped Dardis develop the appearance and structure of the final design. "Some of these images can be very painterly," he explains. "If the accidental color mixing is attractive, the result can be inspiring. If the unintentional colors are muddy, the result can be discouraging. You need to learn how to pick what's going to be most helpful." The effort appears to be well worth it. The complexity and interest of the intermediate imagery are reflected in more complex and interesting final designs. Dardis's experiments are now incorporated in a new course he teaches, dedicated to experimental uses of computers in design process.

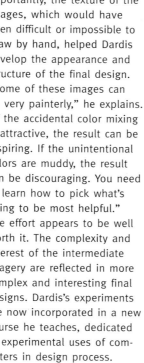

By adding these interesting but abstract images together, he developed what he could interpret as the façade of an office building. The final physical model reflects the imagery developed serendipitously.

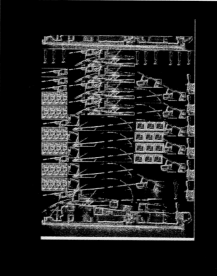

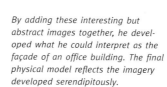

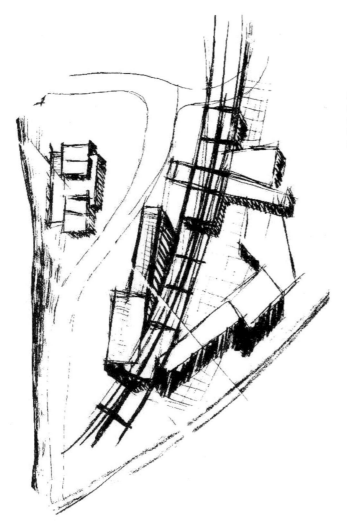

In a second project, Dardis began the
design of a forest-research complex with
charcoal sketches of a site plan that
included preliminary ideas about the
buildings and the spaces between them.

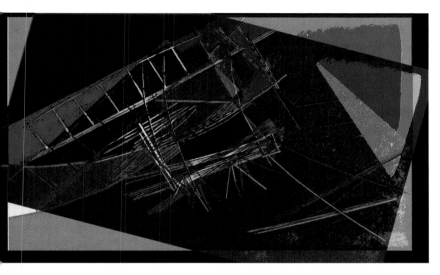

Dardis scanned a physical site model
based on preliminary sketches and
performed a series of computer manipulations on the resulting images.

Among the computer manipulations
Dardis was startled to discover an
unintended resemblance between one
resultant site plan and a charcoal
sketch he had done earlier of a
building section.

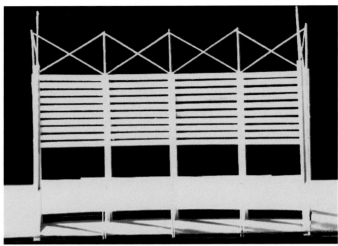

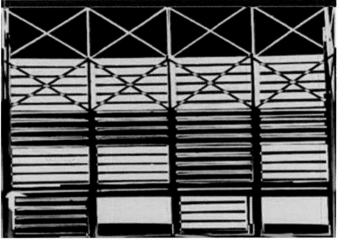

To develop ideas about the façade of
one of his research buildings, Dardis
began by building a small bench from
balsa wood and editing the image.

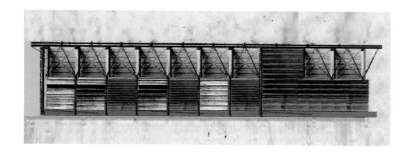

A scanned model of multiple bays, edited and merged with images originating with the bench, went through a series of modifications and ended, finally, with a developed idea for the building's façade.

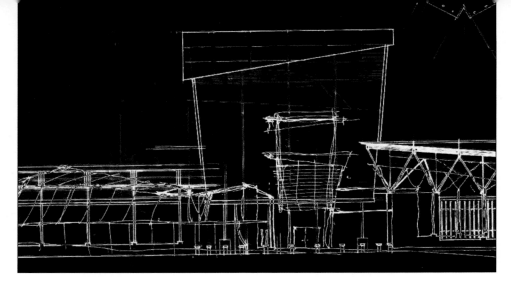

*Sketched ideas about a building's
main entrance went through a series
of manipulations including hand
sketches, manipulations of the scan,
and hard-lined drafted renditions.*

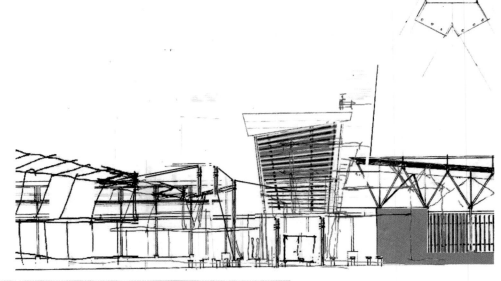

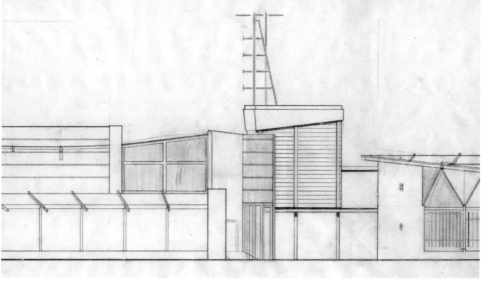

The final image for the building entrance demonstrates a painterly richness that would have been virtually impossible to achieve via a conventional architectural design process.

The broad range of available media and processes is on display in the work of Ross Leventhal, who was an architecture student at the University of Oregon. Professor Kevin Matthews assigned the design problem of a public library for a small town in Oregon. In addition to accommodating library and civic functions, the building needed to anchor an important street corner in the traditional, turn-of-the-century downtown and create a transition to the nearby river.

Library for the Twenty-First Century:
High-Tech Media in a Small-Town Setting

As with any good design, the building would need to provide ample natural light and inspiring but usable spaces. Moreover, in anticipation of a fifty-year life span, the building had to accommodate spatial flexibility reflecting current uncertainty about how the relationship between people and books will change over time. Juggling all these considerations, Leventhal and the other students also needed to think at several scales simultaneously, designing for the town, the street, the building structure, and the detail.

Working with the 3D modeler DesignWorkshop and 2D drawing software PowerCADD, the students selected media appropriate for each phase of their design processes. To begin, they built a collective site model. Each student selected a building in the neigborhood to measure and model; by combining these models, each student had a copy of the entire town in which to develop their own design. Leventhal worked on initial design studies directly in DesignWorkshop, developed a simple massing model that laid out the main spaces. This was like the preliminary bubble diagrams of traditional design processes, except that, because this was a 3D computer model, he was then able to walk through it and examine the effectiveness of the proximities of spaces in three dimensions. A special function within DesignWorkshop enabled him to call up the name and square footage of each area.

For a ten-week studio project at the University of Oregon, architecture student Ross Leventhal designed a library for a small Oregon town. The modeling and photorealistic rendering enabled him to visualize and develop the design to a higher degree than is traditionally possible in short-term student projects.

Later in his design process, Leventhal studied the relationship of the building façade to the adjoining façades on the block. From the modeling software he printed out a section drawing; then, hand sketching with tracing paper, he was able to draw and evaluate dozens of compositional variations very quickly. He also computed the stresses on the dramatic steel structure of the

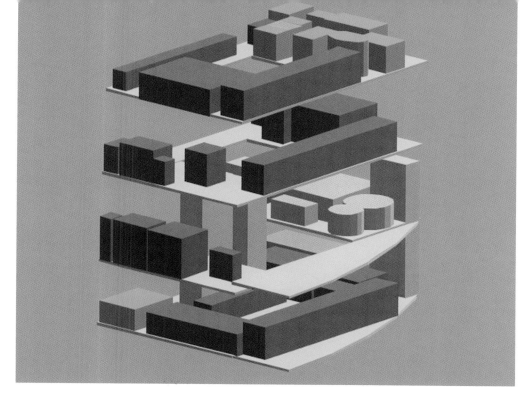

riverfront façade and sized the members with the program MultiFrame. When the design developed to the point where he could assign colors, he created photorealistic renderings with Radiance to determine the quality of light in the proposed spaces. In small-group discussions about the design in progress, Professor Matthews marked up the drawings, both on paper and in 3D within DesignWorkshop, to make suggestions about areas of further development.

Because Leventhal had access to the collectively created site model, he could evaluate his design repeatedly within the context of the entire town as the design developed. At one point late in development, he studied a perspective of his building's Main Street façade as the culminating feature of

the city block. The highly glazed façade worked well in terms of the building's internal organization, the views from the library, and the light it let in. But he quickly realized that the glazed, transparent corner made a less than substantial cornerstone to the block. "It was as if the town had no ending," he recalls. "The massive buildings had created a certain rhythm in the small town, and the glass corner had broken the pattern." Compared to the heavy masonry of the older buildings, his design needed something more massive to end the block. He replaced the corner glazing with an opaque vertical panel and achieved this goal. Without the realism of the computer renderings, he wouldn't have known what was lacking or how to transform it.

The resulting design, though it will never be built, is probably more highly developed than could be expected from student work during a ten-week term without the benefit of computer media. Like the small Oregon town itself, with its anticipation of changing information needs over the next fifty years, the project was a mix of new and old, of digital and traditional media. Young designers entering architecture at the end of the twentieth century bring important understandings to their profession: how to balance the new and old, how to know when to use what tool, and to what end.

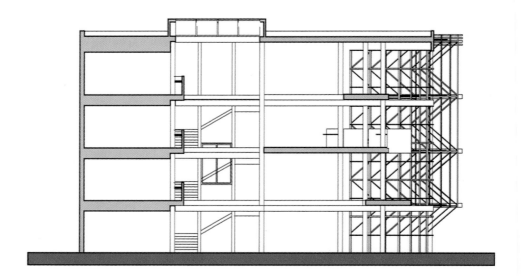

When the building had been modeled in three dimensions, the software generated 2D projections such as this line drawing of the building's cross section. Leventhal used this printout as an underlay for sketching many possible variations for the building's north elevation.

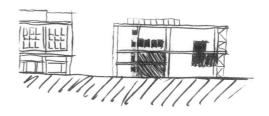

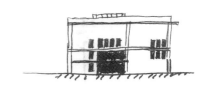

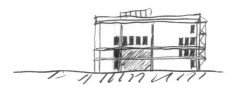

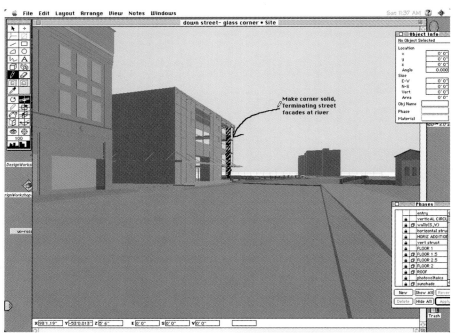

After developing the north façade of his library, Leventhal studied the entire city block in perspective. He noticed that the building's northwest corner, of steel and glass, did not give a solid enough termination to the block. Using the mark-up tools in DesignWorkshop, he and Professor Matthews sketched in a solution that would solidify the corner without changing the character of the building. The final design shows both the resulting street façade in the turn-of-the-century context and the contrasting façade facing the river.

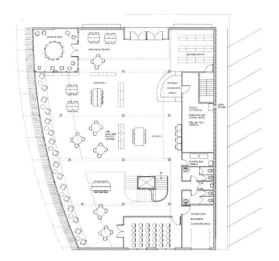

First floor

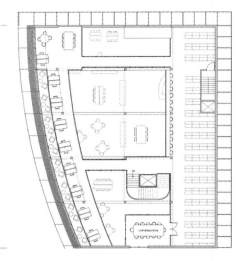

Second floor

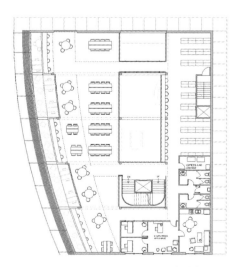

Third floor

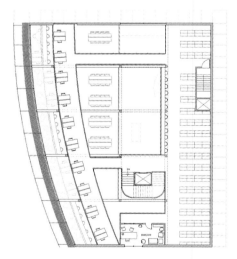

Fourth floor

The completed interior of the small-town library, as designed and rendered by Leventhal, demonstrates how software enables architecture students to visualize the spaces they are developing. Structural detail, spatial characteristics, and light quality and quantity all come alive through photorealistic rendering.

In some studios, conventional assignments are replaced with imaginary design challenges. At the New Jersey Institute of Technology, for example, Professor Glenn Goldman experiments with alternative sources of inspiration for his students. Director of the School of Architecture's Imaging Laboratory, Goldman has been encouraging his design students to use computers for over a decade. Recently he added the innovation of having them design buildings not from a real-life program but from literature.

Drawing from Literature:
Historical and Science Fictions

We've all had the experience of visually imagining the built environments described in books, even those without illustrations. Goldman exploits this imaginative power by asking his students to read books with particularly evocative descriptions and to develop 3D computer models of those buildings and urban environments. These designs must include individual interpretations based on careful readings of the text in order to create a place in which the book's action could credibly take place. "I believe," Goldman says, "that places described in literature can become part of society's collective memory. They take on a sense of reality to those who have read or discussed the work. The line between real and unreal becomes blurred, and sometimes these images become manifest in the architect's real design work." He finds that students working on these projects exhibit more enthusiasm and imagination than they do with more pedestrian problems. Moreover, this is not a temporary change but one that permanently affects how students approach subsequent design projects.

The two imaginary projects illustrated here evoke images of the very old and the futuristic. The City of Desire was modeled by NJIT student Sherri L. Osowski and is based on only a few lines from Italo Calvino's *Invisible Cities*, a fictional telling of the exploits of Marco Polo. Those lines read, "[T]owers rise from its walls flanking seven gates with spring-operated drawbridges that span the moat whose water feeds four green canals which cross the city, dividing it into nine quarters, each with three hundred houses and seven hundred chimneys."

The Arrival Station for the Planet Trantor was modeled from Damian Melo's imagination and is based on the writings of Isaac Asimov. This overhead view of the station shows the densely packed planet surface in the background, punctured by crevasselike streets.

From this sparse description Osowski conjured up an entire town that satisfies the particulars of the description but goes far beyond that. Her town offers the credibility of recognizable settlement patterns while combining historic and modern architectural forms.

From the written description she surmised that the city must be based on an orderly grid. That brought to mind a chess set, and she based much of her subsequent design ideas on the forms of chess pieces and the orderliness of the board. Osowski believes that people with a visual imagination create instantaneous imagery whenever they read. The richness of this imagery enabled her to break out of old habits of insisting on realism and functionality in her design work. "Working on this project definitely loosened me up," she says, and she expects this liberation will continue to feed her imagination even as she works on real-world projects as a professional.

The Arrival Station for the Planet Trantor, modeled by NJIT student Damian Melo, is where travelers first disembark in Isaac Asimov's famous science-fiction novel *Foundation*. The model represents Melo's interpretation of the programmatic elements needed to make this planet function. He not only detailed a monumental and somewhat intimidating edifice but also crafted the landing pads and transportation tubes entered by arriving transport vehicles. These are spaced regularly in what Asimov described as a vast wall, riddled with holes, so big that one couldn't see its top. The entrances lead to the maze-like transit system through the rest of the planet. This wall of tunnels was the first component Melo designed; he then built the rest of the project around them. In *Foundation*, the planet is so densely populated that every square inch of its surface is built up to a height of one mile. "From space," Melo explains, "the planet would look like a smooth,

silver marble, because there's no remaining unbuilt surface. I relate its density and heavy steel construction to New York and Newark, where I live. Only Trantor is built at a much larger scale." Freed by the openness of the program, Melo recalls that he allowed his imagination to take off.

What does this mean for the students' education? Goldman notes, "Through the use of digital media we have an opportunity to better understand the imaginary worlds for what they communicate and the ideas they contain, and therefore create an opportunity to modify our own concept of architecture." Once students experience this liberation of the imagination, they are better able to exercise that imaginative stretch in their professional work.

The students created their models in 3D Studio and 3D Studio MAX. Image manipulation was done with Adobe Photoshop and Micrografx Picture Publisher.

A front view of the Arrival Station shows that every possible building area is exploited in this densely populated planet.

The student's interpretation of landing pods, or parking tubes, for arriving transport vehicles.

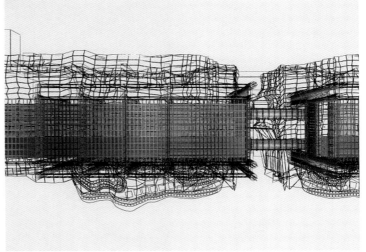

Seen from above and in wire frame, the arrival station displays its structure and the massive rock on which it is built.

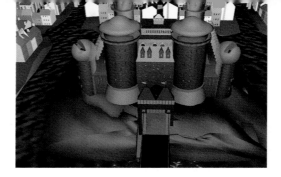

The phrase "towers rise from its walls flanking seven gates" from Calvino's prose provides a framework but leaves plenty of room for interpretation into architectural form.

A dense medieval city surrounding the chess set–inspired castle reminds us that the design images created by reading literature are no less valid for being fictional.

"Four green canals cross the city," says Italo Calvino of the City of Desire in his novel Invisible Cities. *Interpreting a brief passage, Sherri Osowski designed the entire city and its central castle.*

"...three hundred houses and seven hundred chimneys," continues Calvino. Scant input for an entire urban design, yet combined with the student's imagination, it comes to life as a credible city.

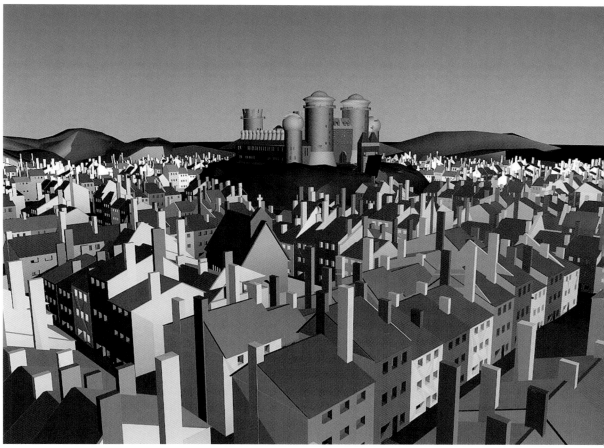

An aerial view of Calvino's City of Desire demonstrates the overall layout of buildings and the traffic links between the canal-divided quarters.

Another architecture professor who draws from literature as a source of ideas for design students is Darlene Brady at the University of Illinois at Urbana/Champaign. Her approach is somewhat different from Goldman's, however, because she emphasizes animation as a presentation medium. "Architecture is a three-dimensional entity," she notes, "that we experience as much through movement as repose."

Light, Motion, and Form:
Drawing Architecture from Books

By developing animations, Brady feels her students achieve a deeper understanding of the buildings they design. Variations in movement, sound, light, color, and materials enable students to express more emotion and abstract ideas than they can through static images. When, as in any design studio, they struggle to integrate expressive forms with the practical concerns of constructibility, the realism of the animation helps them keep track of many issues at once without losing their initial emotional intent.

Several teams of Brady's students submitted award-winning projects to the Graphisoft design competition in 1997. Sponsored by Graphisoft, maker of the architectural modeler ArchiCAD; the American Institute of Architecture Students; Apple Computer; and by *Architectural Record* and other publications, this competition asked students to contribute models of places found only in literature or mythology. Competitors were invited to interpret works that don't actually exist but are nevertheless real in our culture. In the process, they were also asked to explore the potential impact of technology on architectural design.

The imaginary city of Despina was modeled by students from the University of Illinois at Urbana/Champaign. The side of the city facing the sea gives the impression of rock-solid stability; from the desert, it resembles a ship ready to set sail.

One group of Brady's students—Brian Dell, Faiza Malik, and Terence Yan—chose the city of Despina from Italo Calvino's *Invisible Cities*. This fictitious seaside city, perched on a desert shore, has two faces. To those who arrive by sea, it gives the impression of rock-solid stability; for those who arrive after trekking across the desert, it resembles a ship ready to set sail. The students interpreted this dual nature by creating a structure with two very different sides. Both images

are mirages, however, and visitors drawn to these illusions must enter an underground museum to learn the true nature of the city. The animation that the students developed over the course of the design project informed them about where their design was meeting the dual-image objective—and where it wasn't. Recalling their experience on this project, Dell says he and his classmates developed a keener awareness of the potential power of the collective society in improving the quality of urban life. He says, "In architecture we use words to describe places and how a space would feel. For me, architecture now has the opportunity to evoke feelings and emotions as literature does. I now believe that city form and architecture will become one in nature and united in form and function."

Another team of Brady's students—J. Vincent Bates, Elizabeth Milnarik, and Carrie Warner—based their design project on *The House of the Spirits* by Isabelle Allende. Their animation follows a path from subterranean heaviness to soaring weightlessness, representing a metaphoric journey to self-realization by the book's character Esteban Trueba. In describing the house, the students note, "Through a path which begins firmly rooted in the ground, in all that is heavy, dark, and solid, the visitor is drawn through the gradually ascending spaces by momentary glimpses of mysterious, unimaginable shapes, increasing levels of light, and a softening of forms. The metamorphosis of dark to light, heavy to delicate, earthbound to airborne is an architectural representation of the path that Trueba, and through him, all of us, must take to reconcile body and soul."

Fully recognizing that they will seldom, if ever, have a fantasy-based design project in their professional careers, these students believe that this experience will nonetheless affect their future design processes. Working without an ordinary program and without the constraints of a physical model, they found themselves spending a lot of time discussing how their project could express their evolving ideas about the Allende novel. Says Milnarik, "We learned how to distill and communicate intangible concepts in physical form. These lessons will be useful in the future when we attempt to imbue real buildings with similar emotional intangibles, the mark of real architecture."

The students used ArchiCAD for modeling and animations and PageMaker, Photoshop, and PhotoEnhancer to compose the presentation on boards.

Visitors drawn to the illusions of the city
of Despina must enter an underground
museum to learn its true nature.

An animation of The House of the Spirits, *as modeled by University of Illinois at Urbana/Champaign students, begins in a dark, subterranean space.*

As the animation progresses, the path leads up out of darkness through a house that represents a metaphorical spiritual journey.

The upward journey eventually comes to the roof.

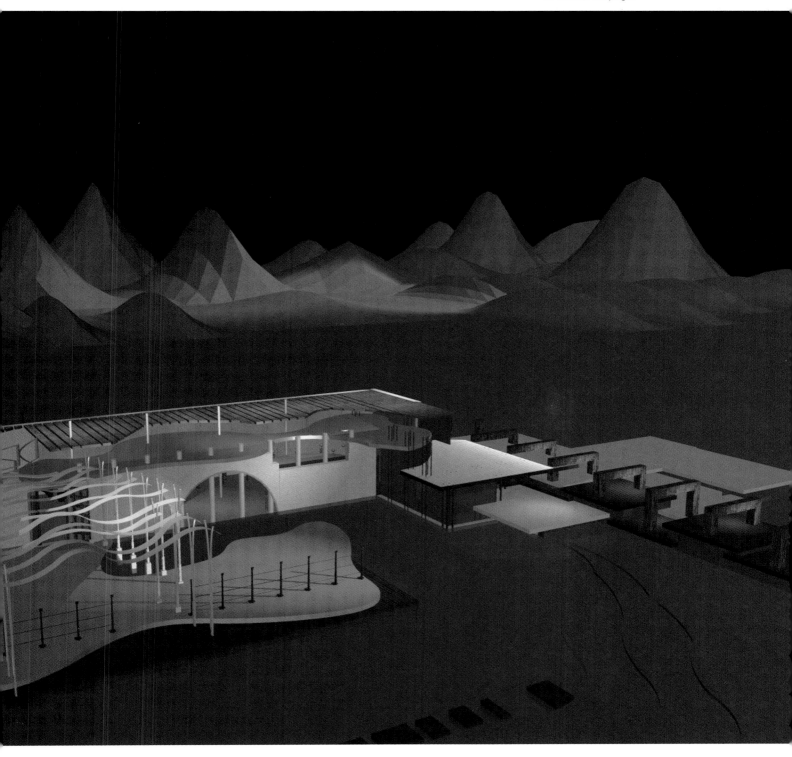

Finally soaring above, we see the House of the Spirits and its surrounding landscape as imagined and rendered by students from the University of Illinois at Urbana/Champaign.

No mortal knows what Asgard looks like, so designing the heavenly home of Norse warrior gods, including Valhalla and other gold and silver halls, is strictly a matter of imagination. When Akos Ignac Ginder, then a student at the University of Belgrade, Serbia, set out on this challenge, he was stretching not only his imagination but the technology he worked with.

Valhalla: The Future Home of Norse Mythology

Ginder, with many other students from around the world, participated in the 1997 Graphisoft Prize Student CAD Competition. Ginder's first-prize winning design of Asgard includes Valhalla, the palace of fallen warriors and chief god Odin; Gladsheim, the golden home of the twelve gods of the Nordic pantheon; and Vingolf, sanctuary of the twelve goddesses. The platform between Gladsheim and Vingolf represents the relationship between the male and female principles, and there sits the pavilion of Frigg, who unites them in marriage. Also modeled are Gimle, the radiant hall that will house the righteous forever, and the rainbow bridge Bifrost, the link between the worlds of the gods and humans. In Norse mythology, the activities of the gods exist in the far distant future, near the end of eternity. Interestingly, though we tend to think of mythological places as ancient, Ginder followed the futuristic theme in his design.

He began by reading everything he could find about Norse mythology. Then he interpreted many of the stories, analogies, and abstractions into architectural form. "Some of the objects," he explains, "represent natural phenomena like the rainbow bridge and the sun-like Gimle. Other objects symbolize mythological characters like the nine Valkyries' towers. While interpreting Asgard, I tried to emphasize the mystical atmosphere which should be present in the home of gods." Though inspired by the stories and the poetry, he notes that total freedom of the imagination is not necessarily a key to design success. In comparing this exercise to a more ordinary, well-defined class assignment, he admits, "Rules are sometimes more inspiring than freedom." Nevertheless, Ginder offers us a glimpse of the end of time, where the final battle between gods and giants, order versus chaos, will play out.

The Norse god Odin passes under the nine Valkyries' towers at the entrance to Valhalla.

Valhalla is the hall where fallen warriors feast with Odin. Seven galleries reserved for chairs of the slain heroes surround Odin's throne, under which a pyramid with a radiant hemisphere represents Odin's one eye, which he exchanged for wisdom.

One of Odin's thrones sits at the center of Valhalla, where the souls of dead heroes are carried by the Valkyries.

Asgard in the long shadows of sunrise.
To the south is the spherical Gimle.

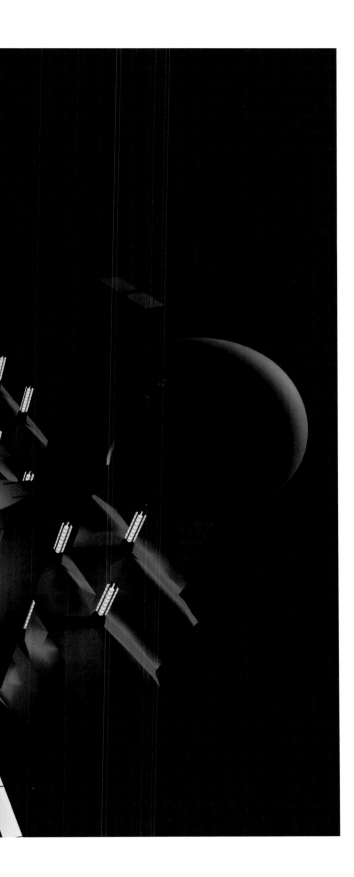

Asgard at sunset features, from left
to right, Bragi's pavilion, with wings
of poetry; Vingolf, the sanctuary of
twelve goddesses; Frigg's pavilion,
devoted to the goddess who presides
over marriage; Gladsheim, where the
gods reside; the nine Valkyrie's
towers; and Valhalla.

The mythological Asgard houses the
Nordic pantheon of gods and goddesses. In Akos Ginder's model, lighthouses
on the field of Asgard symbolize the
constant presence of giants, the gods'
relatives and rivals. Steep stairs and
spiral ramps without railings indicate
that the gods do not die by accident
but by destiny.

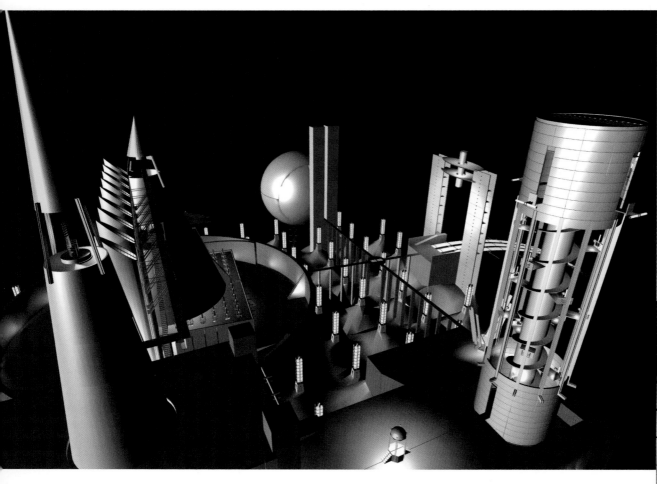

One of Odin's thrones, situated under the golden peak on the top of Gladsheim, represents his position as ruler of the universe.

View from the spiral ramp within Vingolf. Altars devoted to goddesses surround the ramp.

The rainbow bridge, Bifrost, is the road of fire that leads to the entrance of Asgard, the world of gods, from Midgard, the middle world inhabited by humans. At the entrance to Asgard is the watchtower of the guard Heimdal.

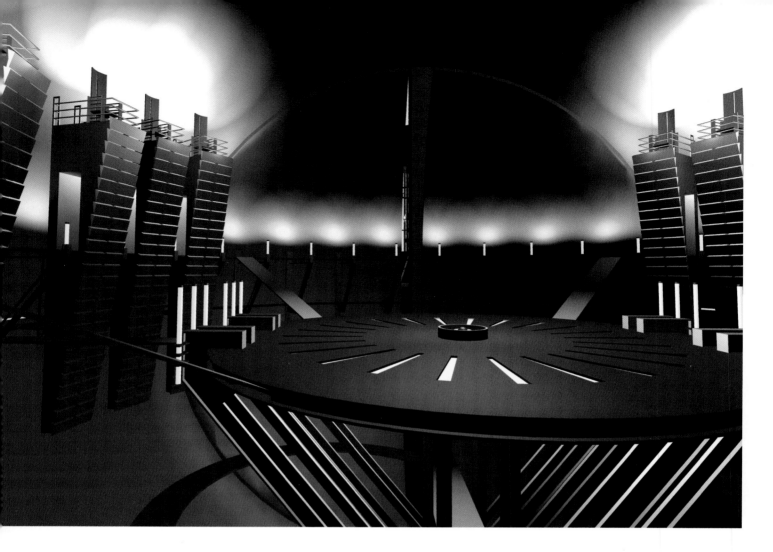

Gimle, the radiant hall of the righteous,
takes on a spherical shape because
of its comparison to the sun. This is
where the sons of gods will gather
after the death of their fathers in the
final battle, and where they will continue to live into eternity. The center
of Gimle is reserved for the bowl of
the giant Kvasir. The bowl is a symbol
of peace and the reunification of the
forces of harmony among the deities.

Twelve thrones are placed inside Gladsheim, the home of twelve gods. Odin, chief of gods, has a throne under the golden peak.

Below each god's throne in Gladsheim is an altar devoted to that god.

Design competitions provide an opportunity for architects and students to experiment with ideas about form and theory. Less constrained by the functional needs of clients or the material demands of getting something actually built, these designers can let their imaginations go. They can create buildings and urban spaces that evoke strong emotions and in the process shake loose the more pedestrian preconceptions of both viewer and creator.

A New Face for Union Square:
Experiments in Urban Form

Such was the goal of San Francisco designers Sean Ahlquist and Meaghan Shinnefield when they submitted an entry to a competition for the redesign of that city's downtown Union Square. Ahlquist describes the existing square as having "bland textures and passive statements on urbanism that fail to coordinate pragmatic functions, while its symmetrical, overly formalized plan describes an uncomfortable space for circulation, occupation, or gathering."

The Ahlquist/Shinnefield design, by contrast, tries to invoke an inventive curiosity among the plaza's inhabitants. The designers relocated an existing monument off to one corner, sculpted the landscape, and designed an open steel structure. This nearly empty scaffolding is meant to mimic the fire escapes, balconies, and construction scaffolds of the surrounding neighborhood. The open metal grating and transparent fabric curtains for walls are intentionally precarious, to grab visitors' attention. At the same time, the structure's openness makes it suitable for multiple purposes—concerts, cafés, farmers' markets, fashion shows; this suggestiveness is meant to encourage visitors to invent their own functions for it.

The tower's metal grating and transparent fabric curtains for walls are intentionally precarious, yet designed to encourage visitors to invent their own functions for it.

On the north edge of the city block, twisting copper walls define the entry and exit paths for the parking garage below. Bougainvillea hedges form barriers between areas for circulation and gathering. Earth berms form grassy pockets for groups of various sizes to congregate; collectively they form a sort of amphitheater oriented toward the scaffolded structure. Ramps of red scored stone rise and fall to create pathways throughout the site. In the middle of the block, a formal, regular, raised elliptical shape offers a contrast to the more chaotic structures. "Our hope," Ahlquist concludes, "was that juxtaposing conventional and unusual forms would hint at new uses for the plaza."

Ahlquist and Shinnefield modeled and rendered the project in 3D Studio Max and 3D Studio Viz.

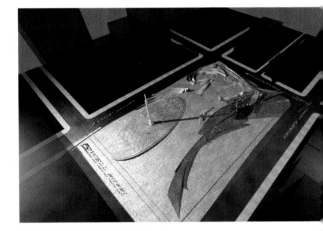

The design included the entire city block, with an existing monument (relocated), sculpted grounds, and the multipurpose tower.

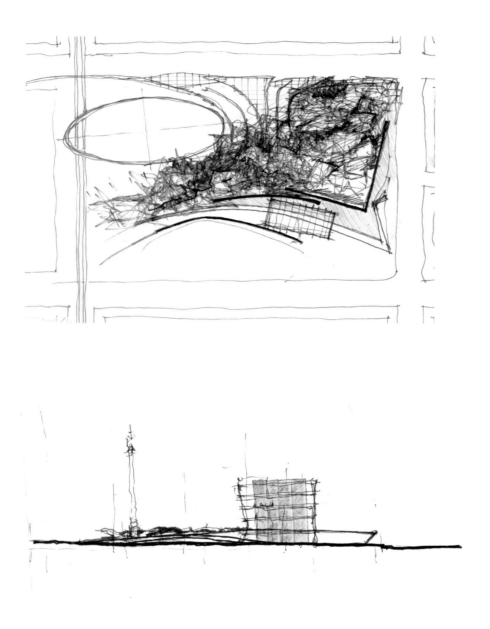

To begin designing, Ahlquist sketched
out ideas in a loose, impressionistic
fashion. As the design developed, he
and Shinnefield shifted to computer
modeling.

An open-scaffold structure was the centerpiece of a redesign of San Francisco's Union Square, developed by Sean Ahlquist and Meaghan Shinnefield for a competition.

The steel structure of the open tower mimics the fire escapes, balconies, and construction scaffolds of the surrounding neighborhood.

Part IV:
Virtual Environments

One of the most interesting new opportunities for architectural services lies in the creation of virtual environments. The term virtual reality (VR) refers to a collection of technologies that help a computer user pretend he or she is immersed in an electronically generated environment. At a minimum, this includes a projection of an interactive 3D model on a computer screen and the user's ability to navigate by moving a mouse or joystick. To add to the sense of reality, the display screen may be projected in stereo images on a head-mounted device, with actions on the screen corresponding to the user's movements of head and hand. Stereo sound can also add to the sense of immersion. With specially prepared 3D CAD models, users can navigate and interact with each other on the Internet. Although most of these environments so far have been produced for computers games, architects and researchers are also seeking more serious applications.

This overview of a corporate cyberspace designed by Peter Anders displays a company's corporate information organized as if it were a physical space.

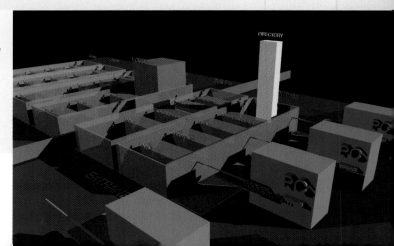

Rooms and objects within Anders's corporate cyberspace correspond to directories, subdirectories, files, and programs. Navigating this virtual building is analogous to finding information in a computer database.

These images show an example of a simulated space built to explain a complex set of information. Michigan architect Peter Anders designed a digital environment to house a company's information systems. This corporate cyberspace, as he calls it, is structured to mimic the flow of information through the company. Regions of the building correspond to computer disk directories, rooms are subdirectories, and the geometric objects in the rooms represent files and computer programs. Users "walk" through this interactive model to find the information they need.

Anders bases his work on the theory that images of physical environments are good analogies that can help people remember detailed information. He cites the "memory palaces" that were invented by orators before books were common. These imaginary collections of rooms served as memory-triggering devices to enable the orator to recall and recite long epic poems, for example, that would otherwise have been impossible to memorize. This ability to visualize space and link it to compartmentalized information is a key aspect of Anders's research. He expects that in the future such environments will help people work productively and protect them from information overload.

The sections that follow present work being conducted at the University of Washington's Human Interface Technology Laboratory. Greenspace II is a place where groups can work collaboratively even though they may be thousands of miles apart. The Flight of the Phoenix conducts a virtual trip to Mars in anticipation of things to come. This small collection of the digital unbuilt is only the tip of the virtual iceberg.

When virtual reality is applied to traditional design practices, the result can be entirely new kinds of communication tools. James Davidson, Dace Campbell, and colleagues at the University of Washington's Human Interface Technology Laboratory (HIT Lab) experiment with virtual environments for small groups. Their Greenspace II facilitates group dynamics among people who are geographically distant yet conducting an architectural design review together.

Greenspace II: A Virtual Environment for Design Collaboration

Although design creativity is often an intensely personal and solitary act, most designs are reviewed by other people at various stages of development. These others may be fellow architects, clients, consultants, builders, and so on. In traditional reviews, the group gathers around a presenter who displays a series of drawings and models to explain the design. As the presenter speaks, he or she uses hand gestures and body language while making connections between the spoken ideas and the drawings. Such interactive design communications are truly multimedia.

In today's global business world, reviews often must be conducted with individuals who are geographically remote from one another. Simultaneously viewing models and drawings via the Internet is helpful, and if the participants are on a telephone conference call at the same time, they can talk about the designs they see. If videoconferencing technologies are brought into play, the participants will benefit from the hand gestures that are so important an augmentation of architects' speech. But how to take advantage of the sense of realism made possible by immersive VR?

The virtual-reality environment Greenspace II was developed at the University of Washington's Human Interface Technology Laboratory. Several users, represented by avatars with abstracted heads and hands, meet in the Greenspace vestibule before beginning their collaborative design review.

Greenspace II incorporates all these capabilities. In this demonstration project, three hotel rooms were modeled and rendered in preparation for the design review. They are connected by a hallway that leads from a virtual vestibule, where users can meet and become oriented to the system. Within the immersive Greenspace II environment, several participants on computers

Three sample hotel rooms were modeled by UW students and are the subject of discussion among the participating architects, who can virtually walk through the rooms.

connected over a network can move within and between the three rooms, study their surroundings, move furniture, and change material colors. To enhance the group dynamics, each participant is represented as a different-colored avatar and is seen by the others as an abstract head and hand. They can also hear each other's speech. A unique aspect of this environment is that each full-size room contains a small-scale model of itself sitting on a table. Participants can gather around the model for discussions, point to different features, and cut cross sections through the model on any vertical or horizontal plane. This corresponds roughly to the ability of traditional design reviewers to point to drawings of the building's plans and sections or to pull apart cardboard models.

Assuming that the participants all have sufficiently powerful computers and fast networks, this interaction can occur nearly instantaneously whether they are in adjacent offices or on opposite sides of the globe. The HIT Lab researchers found that design critics unfamiliar with the technologies require about thirty minutes of navigation before they are comfortable enough with their environment to ignore it and to focus on the design review. Davidson believes that maintaining a connection with traditional communication techniques is essential for these new technologies to be successful in the architecture profession. Because they can overcome many of the limitations of paper media, however, these simulations present a fundamentally new kind of tool for communicating design intentions.

Greenspace II was developed on Silicon Graphics workstations. The geometry for these models was created in AutoCAD with materials rendered in Lightscape and applied as textures using 3D Studio.

On a worktable in each virtual room
are smaller-scale models of the three
rooms so that reviewers can compare
them during discussions.

By touching a box on the virtual
model, a participant can be instantly
transported into an adjoining
virtual space.

Greenspace II participants can cut
cross sections through the scale
models, simulating the kinds of
views common in conventional
design reviews.

With a combination of gestures and voice commands, the participants can move furniture around in a room and change its color.

Long before Sojourner, the little Mars-crawling robot that captured the world's imagination during the summer of 1997, people dreamed of traveling to Earth's nearest planetary neighbor. Actual travel to Mars is years if not decades away, but virtual travel has become routine. Routine, that is, for Seattle schoolchildren experiencing the shuttle Phoenix.

Flight of the Phoenix:
The First Humans Land on Mars

At the University of Washington, researchers at the Human Interface Technology Laboratory created a simulation of a shuttle and its flight. This VR experience enables kids to pilot the shuttle, orbit Mars, land on its surface, and step out onto the Martian landscape. In the process they learn about space flight and interplanetary exploration while communicating and collaborating to solve complex problems.

The Phoenix simulation is unusual in several ways. Most VR simulations exist only as digital imagery on computer screens. The Phoenix also exists as a room-size theatrical stage set built to resemble the electronic model, with control panels on the walls of the shuttle bay and a large console inside the shuttle. Purple lighting simulates nighttime, with yellow accents to represent incandescent lights. The shuttle itself is a sleek, red (Martian camouflage) vehicle with aerodynamic curves; eyelike portals give it the appearance of an eerie alien creature. These elements exist in both the real and virtual environments. Thus, as the children enter the room (shuttle bay) and prepare for the VR experience, they are already becoming familiar with the experimental surroundings. When they don the head-mounted display device, the walls, doors, and panels they see have a physical presence they can also feel. This experience, plus the digital sound effects, further reinforces the sense of reality they perceive. When the virtual shuttle lands on Mars, the stereo imagery is from actual photographs taken during the 1997 *Pathfinder* mission.

The Mars shuttle Phoenix is a virtual-reality environment that teaches school children about space exploration. Designed and built at the University of Washington's HIT Lab, the shuttle model sports a sleek, alien look.

Another asset of the Phoenix is that behind the exciting game-playing and the serious educational aspects lies an experiment in human/computer interaction. By varying the degrees of resemblance between the real and virtual sets, the researchers try to determine an optimum correlation between the two. For example, a real shuttle bay would be chaotic and messy, like any serious

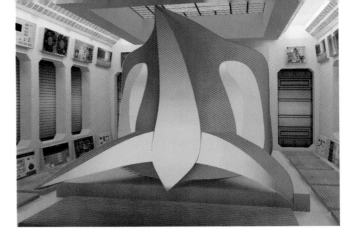

The Phoenix shuttle as it appears from the back. It is positioned to leave the starship and make its flight to the Martian surface. The lighting and wall treatments in the virtual model resemble those of the stage set to augment the sense of reality of the former.

work environment, with oil spills, tools strewn on the floor, and so on.

Such messiness is difficult to model, however, and most computer models appear relatively pristine. What degree of chaos suggested in the physical environment will carry over in the minds of the participants and inhabit the virtual environment? In other words, can a virtual environment benefit from the realism of messiness without the modelers going to the trouble of actually modeling the mess? As the children enjoy their shuttle adventure, the researchers are at work varying the characteristics of the real and virtual environments to determine an optimum combination.

So far, this simulation is a small part of what will eventually become a large project in which twenty to thirty children will be able to participate simultaneously. With networked computers, they will play the roles of flight crew, mission control, and scientists

as the starship explores more of the galaxy. In addition to piloting shuttles and landing on planetary surfaces, they will perform space walks, control remote probes, and operate the command bridge.

Members of the HIT Lab's project Phoenix team are Thomas Furness, Dace Campbell, Susan Tanney, Mark Farrelly, Peter Oppenheimer, and Jon Mandeville. They modeled the Phoenix with AutoCAD, 3D Studio Max, Lightscape, and Alias. The models were then simulated in real time with custom HIT Lab software on a Silicon Graphics Onyx2 Infinite Reality Engine.

As the portal opens and the shuttle prepares for flight, the planet Mars looms ahead.

Appendix A:
Credit and Contact Information

**The Northwest Palace of
Ashur-nasir-pal at Nimrud**
Research by Samuel M. Paley,
State University of New York at
Buffalo, Richard P. Sobolewski
of Warsaw, Poland, and Alison
B. Snyder, University of Oregon

Modeling by Learning Sites, Inc.
Donald Sanders
Learning Sites, Inc.
151 Bridges Road
Williamstown, MA 01267-2232
http://www.learningsites.com/

Pauson House
Modeling by Asli Suner
c/o Karen Kensek
School of Architecture
University of Southern California
204 Watt Hall
Los Angeles, CA 90089-0291

1. Classical Theaters:
Still Playing to
Modern Audiences

Greek theater by
Robert Fabianiak
Paraskenion theater
by Glen Stokes
Theater of Eritrea
by Agata Malczyk
Late Roman Odeum at
Buthrotum by Murray Gilmour

c/o Jerzy Wojtowicz
School of Architecture
University of British Columbia
6333 Memorial Road
Vancouver, BC V6T 1Z2
Canada

2. The Vari House:
Ancient Beekeepers Teach
Budding Archaeologists

Donald Sanders
Learning Sites, Inc.
151 Bridges Road
Williamstown, MA 01267-2232
http://www.learningsites.com/

3. The Mausoleum of Qin:
The Game of Archaeology
Mieczyslaw Boryslawski and

France Israel
View by View
1203 Union Street
San Francisco, CA 94109
http://www.viewbyview.com/

4. Ceren:
A Village Rediscovered

Jenniffer Lewin
Sundance Lab for Advanced
Computing in Design
University of Colorado
Boulder, CO 80309-0314
http://ucsub.colorado.edu/~lewin/

5. The Chetro Ketl Great Kiva:
The Center of the
Anasazi Universe

John Kantner
Department of Anthropology
UC Santa Barbara
Santa Barbara, CA 93106
http://www.sscf.ucsb.edu/anth/
projects/great.kiva/index.html

**6. Santa Reparata,
Santa Maria del Fiore:**
The Evolution of a Cathedral

Christine Smith with
Jude LeBlanc and George
Liaropoulos-Legendre

Modeling and Visualization by
George Liaropoulos-Legendre,
Allen Sayegh, Michelle Tarsney,
Sarah Radding, Markus Schaefer,
Emlyn Altman, Takashi Yanai
Research: Christine Smith,
Christy Collins, Reinerio Faife,
Margaret L. Fletcher, William
Pevear, Markus Schaefer, Scott
Schlimgen. With the collabora-
tion of: Heidi Cron, David
Burnett, Andrea Lamberti,
Irwin Miller, Eric Stark, Takashi
Yanai, Delphine Yip, Anthony
Vermandois

George Liaropoulos-Legendre
Graduate School of Design
Harvard University
48 Quincy Street
Cambridge, MA 02138

7. Cairo:
A City in Flux through Time

Nezar AlSayyad
Center for Middle East Studies
Department of Architecture
UC Berkeley
Berkeley, CA 94720

8. A Mongolian Palace Rebuilt:
Traces of Kublai Khan

Kunio Kida
Taisei Corporation
1-25-1 Nishishinjuku
Shinjuku-ku, Tokyo, 163-06
Japan

9. Tenochtitlan:
The Aztec Capital
Restored to Life

Antonieta Rivera
School of Architecture
University of British Columbia
6333 Memorial Road
Vancouver, BC V6T 1Z2
Canada

10. The Larkin Building:
A Lost Monument
to Modernism

Ken Elwood
School of Building Arts
Savannah College of Art
and Design
P.O. Box 3146
Savannah, GA 31402-3146

11. The Glashaus:
An Experiment
with Color and Glass

Ilaria Mazzoleni, Jennifer
Charleston, and Sarah
Heyenbruch
c/o Karen Kensek
School of Architecture
University of Southern California
204 Watt Hall
Los Angeles, CA 90089-0291

12. The Banff Park Pavilion:
Lost Gem of the Rockies

Brian Sinclair and
Terence J. Walker
Faculty of Architecture
201 Russell Building
University of Manitoba
Winnipeg, Manitoba R3T 2N2
Canada

Part II: Unbuilt Designs of Famous Architects

Trinity Chapel
by Jennifer Charleston

c/o Karen Kensek
School of Architecture
University of Southern California
204 Watt Hall
Los Angeles, CA 90089-0291

13. Reviving Peruzzi:
An Old Master Returns to Fame

Peter W. Parsons
School of Architecture
Rensselaer Polytechnic Institute
Troy, NY 12180-3590

14. A Possible Palladian Villa:
Understanding History
through Technology

Thomas Seebohm
School of Architecture
University of Waterloo
Waterloo, Ontario N2L 3G1
Canada
http://www.fes.uwaterloo.
ca/u/tseebohm/

15. The Legacy of Sant'Elia:
Back to the Future

Midhat Delic
915 W. 22nd Avenue
Eugene, OR 97402

16. Geometry to Live In:
The Unrealized Villas
of Le Corbusier

Jerzy Wojtowicz
School of Architecture
University of British Columbia
6333 Memorial Road Vancouver,
BC V6T 1Z2, Canada
http://www.architecture.ubc.ca/jw/

17. Chernikhov's Constructivism:
Fact or Fiction?

Fantasy 4 by Ivo Valentik
Fantasy 39 by Ajay Mistry, Wayne
Lee, Bob Abrahams, and James
Wu. Fantasy 42 by Jeff Zavitz,
Sandy Chan, and James Wu.
Fantasy 93 by Louis-Charles
Lasnier, Mark Sider, Filip Simpson
and Ari Wahl
Thomas Seebohm
School of Architecture
University of Waterloo
Waterloo, Ontario N2L 3G1
Canada

18. The Illinois Building:
Wright's Mile-High Fantasy

Urs Britschgi, Mike Hsu, Ashley
Schafer, and Max Strang
Graduate School of Architecture,
Planning, and Preservation
Digital Design Laboratory
Columbia University
New York, NY 10027
http://brooklyn.arch.columbia.edu/
DDL/projects/usonia/usonia.html

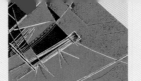

Appendix B:

Software Sources

3D Studio
3D Studio MAX
3D Studio Viz
AutoCAD
Autodesk, Inc.
(800) 964-6432
(415) 507-5000
http://www.autodesk.com/
index.html

Adobe Photoshop
Adobe Premiere
PageMaker
Photoshop
Adobe Systems Incorporated
(800) 833-6687
http://www.adobe.com/

ArchiCAD
Graphisoft U.S., Inc.
(800) 344-3468
(415) 703-9777
www.graphisoft.com

CAD Overlay ESP
Softdesk (Autodesk)
(800) 763-8337
(603) 428-5000
http://www.softdesk.com/
home.html

DataCAD
DATACAD LLC
(860) 677-4004
http://www.datacad.com/

DesignWorkshop
Artifice, Inc.
(800) 203-8324
(541) 345-7421
http://www.artifice.com/

Electric Image
Electric Image, Inc.
(888) RENDER1
(626) 577-1627 x224 or x273
http://www.electricimg.com/

form*Z
RenderZone
autodessys, Inc.
(614) 488-8838
http://www.autodessys.com/

GDS
Informatix, Inc.
81-3-5460-1811
http://www.informatix-
inc.com/index_e.html

Lightscape
Lightscape Technologies, Inc.
(408) 342-1900
http://www.lightscape.com/

MacroMind Director
SoundEdit
Macromedia, Inc.
(415) 252-2000
http://www.macromedia.com/
index.html

MegaMODEL
MegaPAINT
Just in Time Software GmbH
030-315 95 80
http://www.megacad.com/

Micrografx Picture Publisher
Micrografx
(888) 216-9281
http://www.Micrografx.com/

MiniCad
Diehl Graphsoft, Inc.
(410) 290-5114
http://www.diehlgraphsoft.com/

MultiFrame
Formation Design Systems, Inc.
(408) 440-0702
http://www.formsys.com/

PhotoEnhancer
Eastman Kodak Company
(800) 235-6325
(716) 726-7260
http://www.kodak.com/

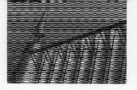

PowerCADD
Engineered Software
(336) 299-4843
http://www.engsw.com/

Radiance
Lawrence Berkeley Laboratory
http://radsite.lbl.gov/radiance/
HOME.html

SoftImage
Softimage, Inc.
(800) 576-3846 #3526
(514) 845-1636
http://www.SoftImage.com/

Specular Infini-D
Specular
(800) 433-7732
(413) 253-3100
http://www.specular.com/

StudioPro
Strata, Inc.
(800) 678-7282
http://www.strata.com/

Wavefront Advanced Visualizer
Alias/Wavefront
(416) 362 9181
http://www.aw.sgi.com/pages/
home/index.html

Index